To Linda Bengtson

She taught me how
She passed it on
She keeps on rolling.

Acknowledgments

Thanks to those who made the book read well:
Top of the list are the scores of lefse makers I interviewed, both on and off the Lefse Trail. They generously gave their time, cheers, tears, stories, reflections, recipes, humor, tips, and invariably their rounds of lefse.

For all my books, I have thanked editor Kathy Weflen, and I hope I always will. I treasure her talent, value her opinion, and cherish her applause. I can sum up our professional relationship with this quote from an email exchange: "Kathy, you're killing me with your questions and requests—but I love you for them! The chapters get better because of them."

I discovered that I thrilled copy editor Shannon Pennefeather Gardner (great name) with, as she wrote, "a few homophones to fix—one of my favorite types of corrections." It's a trick I learned a long time ago, to have a *pear* of homophones handy just to make a copy editor's day. Whenever Shannon returned chapters, she made *my* day by giving the prose a high gloss.

Finally, thanks to Rick Naymark for his writing and marketing guidance. And thanks for the decades-long support of my Friday writers group: John Rosengren, Susan Perry, Jack El-Hai, Cathy Madison, and Tim Brady.

Thanks to those who made the book look good:
Special thanks to Jill Kittock, who elevates this book with colorful, lively, and sometimes lefse-loony illustrations. Her work reflects her person: professional, friendly, and fun. And to Shirley Evenstad, whose rosemaling—along with Bob Olson's woodcarving on one of Shirley's plates—turned my head when I first saw it. I'm not sure if she's better with a brush or with a lefse rolling pin. She makes a good round, don't ya know.

Photographer Tracy Walsh has the gift of making her subjects shine in their own light. She captured the cover image and all the lefse-making beauty shots in the book. I've always seen loveliness in every stage of lefse making, but thanks to Tracy, I finally saw that beauty stop and smile for her camera.

My gratitude to Dan Larson, who created on a lathe the jaw-dropping lefse rolling pin that appears on the cover. And to the Minnesota Woodturners Association for prompting its members to create heirloom lefse rolling pins. I'll give sculptor Paul Olson his due as well. Paul made a lefse-rolling-pin sculpture that proved an artful rolling pin was possible.

Designer Jenny Mahoney took piles of files and a mess of materials and made them into a treasure of a book. Laying out a book is all about "showtime," about taking care of every last detail so when the curtain goes up on your creation, the audience will *ooh* and *aah*. The littlest touches can make a big difference in how the book appears to the reader. With her high standards and low-key style, Jenny took care of every last detail.

Thanks to those who made the book "taste" good:

No, you won't butter and sugar these pages and eat them as lefse. But you're probably hungry to try the 12 original lefse-wrap recipes that chef Merritt Campbell created. I admit you can wrap just about anything in lefse and it will taste good. It's lefse, after all. But Merritt, with help from chef Kate McIntosh, my daughter, made lefse wraps so savory that the stuff inside the lefse *almost* made the lefse second banana. Also thanks to Megan Walhood and Jeremy Daniels of Viking Soul Food in Portland, Oregon, for generously sharing their recipe for a lefse wrap filled with Norwegian meatballs in caramelized goat cheese (gjetost) gravy. Finally, thanks to the lefse-wrap taste testers: Alfonzo and Amaya McIntosh, Laurel and Claude Riedel, John Ziegenhagen, Susan Goll, Paul Olson, Mary Kay Willert, Pat Layton, Brad Engdahl, Leila Mikkelson Preston, Dennis Preston, Anna and David Linder, Sonny Schneiderhan, and Jane Legwold.

Thanks to those who made the book "sound" good:

Composer Erik Sherburne's cranium seems to be a big bowl of melodies. They build up there, so to avoid injury, he drains that bowl daily by dashing off parts or all of a song or six. One of them was "Keep On Rollin'." His melodies and arrangements inspired me to write lyrics, and I appreciate how supportive and patient he was as I threw all sorts of words on the wall to see what would stick. Who knows, maybe we'll collaborate again!

Thanks to Jane Legwold:
I dedicated my first book to her, saying she "has eaten my worst lefse, and my best." She helped make this book my best with her love and unflinching support of me as a writer. Had she ever paused as I pursued a second book on lefse, of all things, there's a fair chance I would have put the book idea aside—and forever regretted it. But she never hesitated in saying, "Go for it." And when I was limping to the end of the book, seemingly unable to look at one more lefse photo or write yet another line about my favorite food, she came riding in, bugles blaring, patting me on the rump and tossing one precious lefse shot after another until we had the right ones. I have written many good things, and the best is yet to be, I believe. And so it is with Jane and me: The best is yet to be. And nothing will ever surpass what I wrote on the inside of the wedding ring I gave her 45 years ago: "See you tomorrow Hon."

Jane Legwold, my wife, has tasted my worst lefse and my best.

Contents

1
Lefse Is a Classy Lady

Lefse is a classy lady,
This we know to be true.

She was there through our uneven youth,
Smoothing, soothing, oh so sweet.

She was there when we were off to ...
Tears and prayers and miss-yous in the pillow package of toasted flour.

She was there when we returned, cavalier and stride full.
She nodded humility at the screen door. "A little lunch, then?"

She was there when we Gave Thanks each year,
Sensual, soft, stunning, dressing up the day ... turning heads at the
Christmas table.

She is there when the old ones go, closing the crackly, weighted black album,
And when the young ones come, blessing their big-eyed, breathless open book.

She is there when we slow and slump and stumble.
She knows ... She knows ... She shrugs and smiles and says, "Keep on rolling."

Lefse is a classy lady,
This we know to be true.

It was February, cold and gray with a raw headwind slowing what promised to be a grim trip from Minneapolis to Northfield, Minnesota. I was bringing lefse I had made that morning to Linda Bengtson in the long-term care unit of Northfield Hospital & Clinics. Linda had taught me how to make lefse nearly three decades earlier.

I was 66 years old, and a couple of weeks earlier I had been laid off from what was probably going to be the last job of my career. Although the layoff was about sweeping company changes and not about my performance, this was not the way I wanted to exit the workplace. What's more, I had not written anything of note for a decade, and I wasn't sure I wanted to—or could—write anything of note. Breakfasts with friends, singing at church, and my grandkids, 8-year-old Amaya and 6-year-old Zo, seemed to be the only things that moved me from my couch. Otherwise, I would sit in sunny silence, reading or trying to write, legs elevated and covered with a blond fleece blanket.

Linda's spouse, Denny Bengtson, my cousin, had emailed in early February that an ambulance had taken Linda to the hospital. She had difficulty swallowing and experienced severe edema and extreme pain stemming from four compression fractures in her back. "Her back must be so brittle and soft due to all the steroids she has taken over 40 years [for her rheumatoid arthritis]," wrote Denny. "Seemingly all she has to do is stretch or twist too far—or even bend over—for it [fracturing] to happen."

When Denny updated the family 10 days later, the news was dire. Their son Nathan was flying home from Seattle, and daughter Brianna was flying from Korea. "She is on a downward spiral—zero appetite and conscious for only short periods of time. Shortly she will no longer be with us. My sense and intuition and hope are it will be soon, in a matter of weeks. Then she will be *free!*"

I parked at the hospital and gingerly gathered the package riding in the passenger seat. Warmth from the lefse created a mist inside the clear plastic bag protecting the rounds. Bearing my offering in both hands, I walked into the lobby. "Linda Bengtson's room, please."

I don't enter hospitals anymore without thinking of the heart attack that occurred when I was 56 and training to run the Twin Cities Marathon. The damage to my heart was slight, and three stents made me good to go, miraculously. In fact, after a couple of weeks of rest and supervised rehabilitation, I slowly resumed training, always checking with my cardiologist and thinking, just maybe, I could do the race. Long story short, I came back and finished that marathon four months after the heart attack.

A visit with Linda Bengtson, my mentor,
prompted me to write my second lefse book.

Linda was alone when I entered her room. She was awake and alert. Her voice was weak but animated as we talked about our favorite subject—making lefse.

"I was 7 or 8 years old when I started helping my mom, Ruth Satren, bake cookies and make lefse," recalled Linda. "It was hard for her hands mixing the dough; her hands were bad with rheumatoid arthritis. She was in her mid-40s then. ..."

Be It Resolved

Before the visit, I had had passing thoughts about writing another lefse book to celebrate 25 years of my book, *The Last Word on Lefse*. Frankly, I wasn't wild about the idea. Writing one book on lefse in a lifetime was probably enough—and, after all, it claimed to be "the last word on lefse." But during this visit, I started to think that maybe, just maybe, I could do this. Maybe I had enough stamina and writing chops left, and maybe I could find ample fresh material in Lefse Land to warrant another lefse book.

Then three events happened in short order that made it all but certain I would write another book on lefse. First, a nurse bearing medications interrupted us. Second, a food server showed up a few moments later and offered chocolate pudding, applesauce, and juice. And third, Linda showed the lefse first to the nurse and then to the food server, and both gave us blank stares. Here in Northfield? In a town thick with Norskies, home to St. Olaf College, these two young women did not know what lefse was?! This reawakened a dormant fear, the very fear that stimulated me to write *The Last Word on Lefse:* that lefse making was a dying tradition. Something had to be done about it!

Linda graciously explained lefse to the nodding nurse. And then later with the food server, Linda pointed and said: "That is lefse. Norwegian lefse. Gary wrote a book about lefse. He is Denny's cousin. He one time called me out of the blue and asked if I could teach him how to make lefse. I said, 'OK, but we have to do this over the phone,' because he lives in Minneapolis. So we did, and he's been the Lefse King ever since. I gave him the job. I didn't want that job any more. He inherited it whether he wanted it or not."

Well, having been crowned by my Lefse Queen—who, I am happy to say, rallied and returned home—I said to myself right then in that hospital room: "Maybe my work is not yet done. If the grand tradition of lefse making is to die, it shall not be during my reign!"

One year before my mother, Elen Stevenson, passed, I sensed that the lefse-making tradition in our family was dying. It dawned on me that, "Oh no—no one else is really learning! We have to keep this going!" It's interesting that as we get older, it hits us and we realize that time is passing.

—Shirley Faa, 67, Minot, North Dakota

2
Really? Another Lefse Book?

I have fond memories of making lefse with my granddaughters, and we're all covered with flour. We're a mess because when we roll, we're not too careful. The sponge cleanup is everywhere in the kitchen, but the mess is part of the fun of lefse.

—Janice Knudson Redford, 75, Cambridge, Wisconsin

The morning after I had resolved to write another lefse book, I was a mess. I realized I had been under the influence of lefse when I made such a commitment, even if it was only to myself. Writing a book is a colossal undertaking. What was I thinking? Clearly, I hadn't been thinking.

At Linda's bedside, I had been in a lefse lather, a lefse zealot stoked by potato passion to ensure that the lefse-making tradition would not only survive but also thrive. I was charging headlong into the book-writing battle without the backing of ideas, events, names, and places to fill the book.

Still, I did have a *few* ideas. I didn't know if they'd amount to much, and maybe I was making too big a deal out of this perceived threat to the tradition.

I cool-headedly decided to plug into my passion and see where the ideas went. What could it hurt? Besides, what else did I have going? That said, I assured myself that if the ideas turned out to be one dud after another, I would pull the plug. The new book had to stand alone, to excite me with imagination and originality. It had to be something more than a rerun.

This decision to go step by step turned out to be excellent, if I may say so. Sure, I had several ideas that ended up being underwhelming, but they were overwhelmed by ideas that were doozies, better than what I expected. Leads led to more leads,

Traveling the Lefse Trail put 8,500 miles on my Prius. Hawk Creek Lutheran Church (see Chapter 21) cemetery is in the background.

ideas begat ideas, and each generation stoked in me an excitement that glowed brighter by the day. *I may be onto something here!* My to-do list lengthened, my fog lifted, my pace quickened, and the number of miles I put on my Prius to visit lefse makers and lefse "shrines" grew to nearly 8,500.

Two main ideas motivated me: to write about the six largest lefse-making plants in the nation, and to talk lefse once again, to hang with lefse makers as they rolled their dough and told their sweet, merry, and moving stories of how lefse formed their heritage and touched their families, especially at the holidays.

The Lefse Trail

I had written about Norsland Lefse and Carl's Norwegian-Maid Lefse (now Carl's Lefse) in *The Last Word on Lefse*, but I wanted to visit all the commercial lefse makers and manufacturers of lefse-making tools and see how they ran their businesses—and especially how the lefse market was holding up.

In Part 1, the Lefse Trail makes 13 stops and visits dozens of hardworking, wily, and colorful characters. It begins in Blair, Wisconsin, at Countryside Lefse, and swings west for two stops in Iowa, in Decorah at Vesterheim Museum and in Cresco at Bethany Housewares. Then it winds its way north through Minnesota with stopovers in Rushford at Norsland Lefse, St. Paul at Northwest Casting, and Osakis at Jacobs Lefse Bakeri. The trail passes through Starbuck, home of the World's Largest Lefse, and Barnesville for the National Lefse Cook-off. It goes to Mrs. Olson's Lefse in Gonvick in northwestern Minnesota, then heads due west for two visits in North Dakota, in West Fargo at Freddy's Lefse and in Minot at the Norsk Hostfest. In Montana, it makes a stop in Opheim at Granrud's Lefse Shack. The Lefse Trail ends in Portland, Oregon, at the Viking Soul Food lefse-wrap food truck.

Learning to Get a Round

My second main motivation in writing *Keep On Rolling* was to talk lefse again. To spark conversation and expand my reach, I ran the following ad for four months in *Viking*, the Sons of Norway national magazine:

For *The Last Word on Lefse,* lefse makers were skeptical when I approached. "How can you write a whole book about lefse?" they'd typically ask. Not so now. Scores of lefse makers enthusiastically responded to the ad. Everybody, it seemed, had a lefse story to tell and was eager to weigh in on the State of the Lefse Union and on the future of lefse making. Yes, they would certainly arrange for in-person interviews while they made lefse! Or if the interview couldn't be in-person, they'd set aside time to chat over the phone. Record the interview? No problem. Send photos and videos? *Yabetcha!*

Gloria Fetty carries a sling of lefse. She was one of scores of lefse makers eager to weigh in on the State of the Lefse Union.

Wonderful stories and lefse-making tips from lefse makers across the nation are sprinkled throughout the book and appear most prominently in the three chapters of Part 2. Their voices create the Lefse Chorus that presents perspective, humor, and even what is heresy to many traditional lefse makers.

Above all, the Lefse Chorus rolls out round after round of practical advice on having fun while making superb lefse.

Final Rounds

With tales from the Lefse Trail and the bounty of responses from the Lefse Chorus, I felt there was *almost* enough for a book—at least a book I could wholeheartedly get behind. But to seal the deal, I needed something extra, something exceptional. I wanted to talk lefse again, but I didn't want the conversation to end after Christmas Day. What could keep the conversation going?

I found four answers. Two came by chance on the Lefse Trail (ah, the trail offers many unexpected treasures), and two came from leafing through *The Last Word on Lefse*. Part 3 elaborates on these lefse innovations:

This Danish ham-and-cheese lefse wrap is one of a dozen lefse-wrap recipes developed by chef Merritt Campbell.

1. "It's a Wrap—A Lefse Wrap!" (page 220). The success of the Viking Soul Food lefse-wrap food truck challenged me to come up with a half dozen or so original, mouth-watering lefse wraps. Well, Merritt Campbell, a chef at the Lakewinds Food Co-op in Richfield, Minnesota, developed the dozen found in Chapter 19. Use these to host lefse-wrap taste-testing parties and shorten your winter.

2. "Make an Heirloom Lefse Rolling Pin" (page 242). I was reminded how striking a lefse rolling pin could be while rereading *The Last Word on Lefse*. I saw Alice Miller's breathtaking walnut pin made in Norway in the 1800s and thought, *How can I make such a beautiful pin?* I challenged the members of the Minnesota Wood-turners Association to fire up their lathes and turn the most artful and yet functional lefse rolling pins they could imagine. Not

only did they come through big-time in Chapter 20, but also one of their members, Dan Larson, developed simple plans so that beginning woodturners (you?) can make a gorgeous pin. Larson made that beauty of a pin that graces the cover of *Keep On Rolling.*

These lefse rolling pins and this lefse stick are the creations of Minnesota Woodturners Association members.

3. I had heard of "The Holy Roller" (page 256) several years ago and then kept hearing his name while traveling the Lefse Trail. Even before lightning struck in 2016 and burned down Hawk Creek Lutheran Church in rural Sacred Heart, Minnesota, the Rev. Dan Bowman, the church's pastor, was gaining small-town fame by connecting faith with lefse. He rallied a sleepy congregation to make and sell lefse as a fundraiser for the church in 2008. The congregation responded to his leadership; he rolled lefse like a machine, and he used his "Lefse Catechism" and his saw and violin bow to spread the word in music and speeches. The church had slowly grown as the fall lefse-making grill-and-sell campaigns got bigger and better each year. And the 2017 campaign has special meaning as the Hawk Creek congregation hopes to have a

The Rev. Dan Bowman, aka the Holy Roller, connects faith with lefse and keeps his church rolling.

new church standing come Christmas. Chapter 21 tells how this prairie preacher with a passion for lefse has made a difference.

4. "An Original Lefse Song" (page 270). The last page of my first lefse book offered the lyrics to arguably the most famous lefse song: "Just a Little Lefse Will Go a Long Way." So why not stick to form with *Keep On Rolling?* Why not commission a new song about lefse, resiliency, tradition, and lasting family values? A tall order, to be sure, but St. Paul composer Erik Sherburne was up for it when I asked. Neither of us wanted another corny lefse song; there are plenty of good ones already. We wanted something more reflective, but still fun. Something we'd want to sing while rolling, which in a roundabout way helps in making good lefse. We wanted a song that could serve as an anthem for the Lefse Chorus and all those who honor the lefse-making tradition. The result, titled "Keep On Rollin'," makes its debut in Chapter 22.

I like to think of this book as a reflective ramble, a walk taken for pleasure with special friends. It's a tour of past, present, and potential future encounters with the lefse culture. Let's get rolling!

*Who comes to mind when I'm making lefse?
Probably my grandmother. She always wore
a red or yellow bandana in her hair.
She didn't want hairs in her lefse, and she'd make
us wear bandanas so we'd all look the same.
Ah, those bandanas—and the fancy homemade
aprons made on her treadle sewing machine!
I still have some of those aprons.*

—Brenda Brown, 53, St. Francis, Minnesota

Part 1
The Lefse Trail

3
Blair, Wisconsin

Never give up. Lefse making can be tough.
You can get tired, but don't give up until it's all
done. It helps to be a little crazy. We made 10
batches [620 rounds] a couple of weeks ago, and
we were all half dead by the time we were done.

—Susan Slinde, 77, Stoughton, Wisconsin

The Lefse Trail begins in Blair, a small town 14 miles west of
Interstate 94 and tucked in the wooded, rolling hills of western Wisconsin's Coulee Region. The Lefse Trail beckons us off
the beaten path. Once we're off the interstate and onto two-lane
roads, the slower speeds tend to unravel the knots in our shoul-

ders and our thinking. We sense we have more time, not less, and possibilities are on the horizon.

Entering Blair (pop. 1,379 in 2013) from the east on State Highway 95, I passed Lake Henry, which is the result of damming the Trempealeau River. Most of Blair's people are descendants of Norwegians who settled here in the 1850s. Dairy farms dominate the area, and the four-day Blair Cheese Fest in mid-September pulls in people from all over the region.

Countryside Lefse Co. employs 15 to 20 locals, depending on the season, and in 2015 celebrated its 50th anniversary. I'll posit, with bias and without evidence, that the near doubling of Blair's population since 1950 was all about lefse. Who wouldn't want to live in a town with a lefse factory?

I turned off my Google Maps app in Blair. How hard could it be to find a lefse factory in a small town? I drove all around the vibrant downtown and finally had to ask. A man pointed west on East Broadway Street. "Can't miss it," he said.

I pulled up to a blue metal-siding warehouse with a tower of gnomes in front. Hanging on the outside wall of the 7,500-square-foot building was a neon-green sign with red letters declaring: HELP WANTED.

Countryside uses 250,000 pounds of potatoes yearly.

How It's Done

Countryside's affable owner, Marshall Olson, 59, impressed me as a busy man who made time for anyone wanting to talk lefse. He stated what all commercial lefse factory owners on the Lefse Trail would tell me: Finding employees was the fundamental challenge, especially for him. Countryside distinguished itself from all the other commercial lefse makers I spoke with by selling hand-rolled lefse made from real potatoes. Other factories used real potatoes, he said, but machines rolled or assisted in rolling. Or the factory used only people to hand roll the lefse, but its recipe had instant potatoes.

Making lefse is arduous, sometimes seasonal work that doesn't attract many young people. Some employees, like Darlene Wagner, who had worked for Countryside for 30 years, were nearing retirement or had retired but worked part-time. Some made lefse as a second job. Some started work but stopped because the job messed up their unemployment or disability payments. Some took the job and then quit when the going got tough. One owner (who wanted to remain anonymous) said he fled the business because workers were eager when the lefse season began, but bailed when things went bonkers in December. That left him frantically scrambling to find any warm body to work around the clock in order to meet the manic, must-have-lefse-for-the-holidays crowd.

Countryside Lefse
makes up to 5,000
rounds of lefse
in a day.

I interviewed Olson in the lobby. A "Busy Making Lefse" sign hung on the wall behind the counter. Looking through a window into the lefse-production room, I could see women rolling out dough (rolling lefse always steals the show).

The room had fluorescent lighting, a tall ceiling, and 50-pound bags of all-purpose flour stacked here and there. About a dozen women in hairnets stood at their stations on flour-covered perforated rubber mats. Flour covered the rolling tables, and two women at each table rolled lefse. The women started with a half cup of dough, made just a few passes so the dough was oblong, flipped the lefse, and finished the round with a few more passes. They were strong and sure and fast, rolling out two or three expansive 17- to 19-inch rounds a minute. As the lefse flopped onto the hot grills, the rounds brought to mind broad-winged stingrays gliding in the ocean.

The three long gas grills were arranged to form a U, abutting the rolling tables. Each grill could hold nine rounds. One worker per grill turned the rounds with a lefse stick, and then she lifted the finished lefse onto a cooling rack. Olson made the 4-foot-wide wood racks by attaching two rectangular blocks with eight dowels.

Finally, workers cut and packaged six large triangles into each plastic bag. Countryside distributes most of its lefse in a 70-mile radius around Blair, but it serves mail-order customers nationwide, shipping in quantities of 6, 12, or 24 packages.

5,000 Rounds a Day

Again, lefse is hard labor. It's work to prepare, roll, and grill just one batch of dough, about 15 rounds. "Now try making 5,000 rounds a day, which we do some days," Olson said. "We use 250,000 pounds of potatoes a year, and we bake year-round. Hand rolled. Real potatoes. Not many commercial lefse makers do that. But today [in September] we're only working three or four hours. It's too hot. I try to keep it upbeat around here. We'll have trouble in November and December because everybody gets tired. There's lots of stress, and we're pushing it out. But January comes, the load comes off, and we relax."

Marshall Olson, Countryside's owner, stands next to lefse-cooling racks he made. He says his business has doubled in the past 20 years.

Olson can give you an earful about the nonlabor issues he's faced: government food-safety regulations; equipment breakdowns; the dwindling number of distributors that dominated the lefse market; accounts that wouldn't pay; and store managers who displayed Countryside's lefse where it spoiled quickly or chose other brands with more preservatives, less flavor, but a longer shelf life.

And yet, even with the challenges and long hours, Olson wouldn't trade occupations with anyone. He is a lefse maker. Always has been. Always will be.

Lefse in His Blood

Olson's parents, Ronnie and Bernice Olson, were farmers who in 1965 started the business in the basement of a drive-in café they owned on U.S. Highway 53. "In '65 most people in this area made their own lefse," said Olson. "They didn't buy lefse. But someone in the family probably said, 'Hey, we should do this.' In the Olson family, we just did it. We weren't afraid to try businesses."

The business slowly grew, and regional groceries such as Robbe's Store in Strum, Wisconsin, started carrying Countryside's lefse. Women were increasingly entering the workforce and appreciated Countryside's quality and the convenience of store-bought lefse.

Olson attended college and was a driver for Countryside. He thought about running a bowling alley/nightclub, but lefse making was in his blood. He bought the family business over time and finally became owner in 2015. He faced his biggest challenge—three years without income—when a January 2003 electrical fire destroyed the former meat locker that had served as Countryside's plant since the late 1960s. The new factory at its current site opened in October 2003.

The new plant was larger than the meat locker and had a better layout, which increased efficiency. "In the last 20 years, we've had steady growth and business has doubled," said Olson. "The truth is we're not really into growing much. We just like to keep customers we have and maybe add something that comes in and fits pretty well. Say a big company came in and wanted 10,000 cases. We'd have to give it lefse we'd normally give to our regular customers. We wouldn't do that because the next year the big company could say it didn't need 10,000 cases anymore. We look for customers that are tuned in. Do they know what our product is, or do they just want something that says 'lefse' on the package?"

Three Parting Tips

Olson said demand for lefse may surpass the supply of lefse makers in the next 10 years or so, and Countryside may have to go with "robotics or some type of machine roller that won't stick," he said. "These machine rollers that some factories use, you've got to flour the heck out of them to prevent sticking. But our dough is so tender that you can't use a machine on it. It would stick. It requires a lot more touch, so we hand roll our lefse."

Olson gave a demo, rolling a round and emphasizing the importance of good dough. "With the right mix, the dough starts forming itself," he said. "If the dough is crappy, that ball is going to go in different directions and stretch too thin." **TIP: "You want thin but not paper-thin, which usually means dry."**

As he finished rolling a round that could cover the top of an oil barrel, Olson pointed to the edge of the lefse. "If this were bad dough, that edge would be ragged. But here, you see, I've got a nice round edge." **TIP: "We always watch the edge; if it's ragged, the lefse is probably going to be dry.** *Good dough makes a good edge.* **A good edge looks pretty, but, more importantly, it's a sign the lefse will be moist and taste good."**

Olson offered a few lefse packages as a parting gift. I asked about the soybean oil listed in the ingredients. **TIP: "We use soybean oil not for taste, which comes mostly from potatoes, but to help the dough mix,"** he said. **"Good dough comes from experience, from feel."**

Driving home, I pondered this possibility: Perhaps using soybean oil in my recipe would strengthen the dough and make it more malleable, easier to roll out and to maintain a good edge … perhaps.

Live and learn on the Lefse Trail.

I enjoy lefse and I enjoy life. It's a lot of work, but it's worth it. Making lefse is a lot of work. It's a chore.

–Janet (Larson) Spracklin, 60, Sidney, Montana

MAKING CHRISTMAS DINNER FOR 70–AT AGE 88

When commercial lefse factories like Countryside Lefse opened in small towns like Blair, Wisconsin, traditionalists feared families would stop making their own lefse. But nearby I met one local family that has kept on rolling–as much for the family fun as for the lefse. I visited 88-year-old Joyce Schmidt and family in Strum, 24 miles north of Blair.

Schmidt's daughter Karen Hanson greeted me. Schmidt was rolling like mad with help from Karen; Judy Foss, the oldest of Joyce's eight children; and Jim Gullicksrud, Joyce's eldest son. Karen had answered my "Wanted: Lefse Makers" ad in *Viking* magazine. She thought her mother would be the perfect interview.

We settled into the morning with Judy, a retired teacher, talking about teaching lefse in her high school Scandinavian Studies course. Jim said he loved lefse best wrapped around side pork (thick bacon). Karen tried to convince us that she was the shy one in the family "who couldn't do anything." Big brother called for a group hug, failing to keep a straight face when he told Karen, "You're valued."

All the while Joyce was relaxed and rolling away. She seemed spry, I thought, and didn't look or move like an 88-year-old. What a treasure these matriarchs are. I had the notion that as long as she kept on rolling, her family felt that, all in all, the world was OK.

"We thought you were short," Karen blurted out to me as the lefse pile grew. I'm 6-0, and I laughed at her candor. "We worried you would be really snooty and serious, and we wouldn't have fun and wouldn't have answers," she said. "And of course, if everything didn't go well, *I* would never hear the end of it from these guys."

I asked Joyce to tell me her lefse story. Soon after she married, she learned to make lefse from her mother-in-law, Hilda Gullicksrud, who sold lefse and donuts. Schmidt went on to have eight children, but when she was 42, her husband, Lawrence Gullicksrud, died of brain cancer.

Over the years Schmidt managed to cook, raise kids, and run the farm. Her second husband, Bob Schmidt, passed away in 2016.

Lefse was a constant through it all. So was the tradition of preparing Christmas dinner for 70 family members—by herself. The menu: fresh ham roast, mashed potatoes, gravy, scalloped corn, warm applesauce, and candied carrots.

Joyce Schmidt, center, still rolling after all these years, is joined by daughters Karen Hanson, left, Judy Foss, right, and son Jim Gullicksrud.

"She *still* makes the whole dinner for all of us," said Jim.

"One year my sister and I thought we should do the meal," said Judy. "It was not right. Mother said the brothers complained. So she shoved us out of the way, and has kept on doing it ever since."

"Wait, at age 88, you make Christmas dinner by yourself for 70-plus people?" I asked, incredulous.

"And I've added rommegrot (cream mush)," Joyce said, rolling her last round.

"Plus her Christmas baking," Karen said.

"I made the trilby cookies, sandbakkels, krumkake, fattigmand, berliner kranz, and lefse for Thanksgiving and Christmas, either the day of or the day before," said Joyce.

Pulling off my visit was a piece of cake, apparently; Schmidt had prepared 10 pounds of potatoes for lefse rolling and then served a wonderful Sunday-gathering type of meal for seven.

Schmidt showed me her lefse pin. "I got this as a wedding gift 72 years ago," she said. "But it's not a keepsake."

Karen protested. "I'd say it's a keepsake! Mother, can I inherit it when you don't want to make lefse anymore? I mean, Judy got–"

"You know what?" Jim interrupted. "I think I got Grandma Hilda's rolling pin!"

"I'm sure," pouted Karen playfully. "*Everybody* gets things before me."

4
Decorah, Iowa

VESTERHEIM

The first time I ate potato lefse, I thought the makers just didn't know how to make the right kind of lefse. We once went to Nordic Fest in Decorah, Iowa, and went all over that town looking for flour [hard] lefse. They looked at us like, "What do you mean?" They didn't know about our kind, and we learned about potato lefse.

—Carolyn Yorgensen, 67, Ames, Iowa

If forced to choose one place on the Lefse Trail not only to get lefse year-round but also to "get it"—comprehend lefse and all else that's rolled into your Norwegian heritage—you could argue convincingly that *the* place is Decorah (pop. 8,089 in 2013). In fact, Eunice Stoen, a lefse luminary featured in *The Last Word on Lefse,* said something years ago that still applies. She told me that many Norwegians touring the United States are drawn to Decorah: "They look around and say, 'You're more Norwegian here than we are.'"

Now, Decorah is not all Norsk. It has a 200-foot waterfall called Dunning Springs, the Decorah Fish Hatchery, the 11-mile Trout Run Trail for cyclists, an ice cave, two breweries and a winery, and the Seed Savers Exchange, which safeguards heirloom seeds. So take in as much of this Iowa bluff-country town as you can. But *oh for sure* see Luther College, Nordic Fest, and the Vesterheim Norwegian-American Museum.

Nordic Fest

Ah, the memories I have of riding with my wife, Jane Legwold, my son, Ben, and my daughter, Kate, on the back of a red convertible in Nordic Fest's Grand Parade. We smiled and waved at people, who also smiled and waved—and squinted at the sign on the car door identifying us—wondering who the heck we were. Well, we were honored guests following publication of *The Last Word on Lefse.* That book detailed the adventures of such legendary Decorah lefse makers as:

Eunice Stoen. Euny once mailed a dozen rounds to actresses Arlene Dahl and Celeste Holm, who wanted lefse for their Christmas dinner party in New York City.

Ida Sacquitne. During the Bicentennial the Smithsonian Institution declared Ida the Great "a national American treasure for her skills in Norwegian-American cooking." She once made lefse for the king of Norway and was still rolling strong at age 90 when she and I made lefse in her cozy apartment.

John Glesne. He regularly demonstrated lefse making at Nordic Fest, which began in 1967. One year he did a demo during the early-afternoon shift on a scorching day. Two women watched his every move, dubious that a man could roll lefse. Sweat dripped off the end of his nose onto the round he was rolling. "The ladies just stood in front and shook their heads," said Glesne, laughing.

Decorah is still home to stars who shine on the many lefse stages spread throughout Nordic Fest, which runs annually on the last weekend of July and attracts 50,000 to 75,000 visitors. So try to catch their lefse shows while you enjoy the bands, jugglers, arts-and-crafts exhibits, bunad show, puppet shows, Scandinavian food booths, lutefisk-eating contest, canoe race, rock-throwing competition, dancing, costumes, fun runs, and fireworks.

Vesterheim

Lefse can be a gateway to a comprehensive understanding of Norway's history and Norwegian-American ways. If you go through that gateway, sooner or later you'll visit Vesterheim. With more than 33,000 artifacts and 12 historic buildings, Vesterheim has the most extensive collection of Norwegian-American artifacts in the world. Founded in 1877, it is the nation's oldest museum about any single ethnic immigrant group.

Such magnificent museums can be overwhelming, so going into my appointment with Laurann Gilbertson, Vesterheim's chief curator, I was singular in my purpose of seeing—and hopefully holding—artifacts pertaining to lefse. After an hour at a computer sorting though hundreds of catalogued items, I had my must-see list of 98. I tugged on blue nitrile gloves to protect museum objects from skin oil and joined Gilbertson in a treasure hunt.

Only a portion of Vesterheim's artifacts is showcased in the main museum, and many items on my list were in the nearby Bauder-Landsgard Collections Study Center. We entered the center and I turned on my recording app to capture Gilbertson's expert interpretations as we moved through the ingenious high-density mobile shelving system.

Gilbertson spoke about each item pulled from the shelf. I, a person of words, was limited to *ooohs* and *aaahs*. Who knew there could be so many sizes and shapes and quirky designs to lefse pins? Slack-jawed, I beheld and, yes, *held* one holy grail of lefse after another!

Laurann Gilbertson, Vesterheim's chief curator, shows an 1838 lefse pin with grooves worn away.

These things were *old*. The description of one 1838 pin read, "Now worn beyond any sign of corrugation at many places near center. Indicates this type rolling pin must have been considerably used in America."

One pin was solid steel, and another was a cobalt-colored glass bottle, shaped like a rolling pin. "You could fill it with cold water to help keep the dough cool," Gilbertson said. Several pins—including one hand-cut and dated circa 1855—had only horizontal grooves.

Many lefse pins had intriguing descriptions. Sigrid O. Melloh, whose father arrived in Brooklyn (presumably from Norway)

Glass rolling pin, circa 1881.

Lefse pin, circa 1855.

Lefse pin,
1800-1830.

Lefse pin
originated in Norway.

around 1901, donated one pin dated 1800 to 1830. "Sent for his wife," said the description. "She was stuck for hours at Ellis Island because she could not understand the immigration official's pronunciation of her name." The wooden pin was found in good condition in Beloit, Wisconsin. The note about the pin said: "From donor's maternal ancestry, Aga, Hardanger [in Norway]." It had turned, teardrop-shaped handles and deep grooves around the pin and along the length. At 22½-inches, it was 6 inches longer than the standard lefse pins used today, indicating that lefse makers rolled larger rounds back then because they cooked lefse on stovetops or hearth plates that were larger than the 16-inch Bethany electric grills used today.

B.C. Wildnes or B.C. Vilmo (apparently the penmanship was poor) donated a pin dated around 1930. According to the description, the woodturner "made about 200 of these rolling pins annually for an American wholesale hardware company." The pin was donated in 1950, and its place of origin was Gonvick, Minnesota. Fine craftsmanship was on display with loose, turned handles and grooves around and along the 20¼-inch length.

"Horse Hoof" Masher

We finished the rolling pins, and I kept pace with Gilbertson as we powered through the rest of the artifacts on my list: lefse sticks, trivets, pastry-board covers, grain-and-coffee grinders, flour brushes, and an 1890 Sveinung Aanondson oil painting with this description:

"girl in Norwegian costume sits by an open corner fireplace in a log dwelling making lefse. Light falls on her face from an open window in an otherwise dark interior." Aanondson (1854–1919) was a Norwegian painter from Rauland, Telemark, and Asgardstrand.

Then there was a 1993 Harley Refsal basswood-and-oak sculpture of a peasant rolling lefse on a wooden table. On the table was a bowl with a heaping

Basswood sculpture of peasant woman rolling lefse.

mound of dough, enough to keep the woman rolling for a long day. The figure, 8 inches high, 8 inches long, and 4½ inches wide, had "Lefse" stamped on the bottom and was done in flat plane carving. In the description's notes section, the woodcarver/sculptor wrote, "deceptive simplicity is the heart of flat plane carving ... a minimalist style ... saying more with less, telling a story with the fewest possible strokes."

One of the day's highlights was meeting my old friends, the wood-turned potato mashers. Photos of six of these mashers appeared in my first book 25 years ago, and I had called them "objects of art," based on what appeared in those old black-and-white images. Ah, but to hold them after all these years! They were even more beautiful than I imagined, and their long,

"Horse hoof" potato masher.

gracefully curved handles anchored to pretty pestle bases gave them personality. I clutched what had been my favorite, the one I had named the "horse hoof" potato masher because its base looked like a horse's hoof. It was just over a foot long, with an angled handle and a curved, smooth finial that was crafted to fit comfortably in the palm. Made by Peter Christenson of Sedan, Minnesota, and found in Glenwood, Minnesota, it was the perfect blend of beauty and function. ... Give me a moment, please.

Two objects brought home the priorities of those leaving Norway. One was a heavy iron hearth plate, 27 inches in diameter, used for cooking and for grilling lefse and flatbread. I said I couldn't imagine lugging this plate across the ocean. "Yes, these were brought to America by immigrants," said Gilbertson. "They felt these plates were too important, that they didn't want to do without them."

The other was a bentwood box for carrying flatbread and lefse. Often these boxes were adorned with rosemaling, but this one had a zigzag pattern that was not just for looks. "A zigzag motif was believed to protect the contents," said Gilbertson. "Because a zigzag was a moving up-and-down symbol, it was believed to

Bentwood box, for carrying lefse.

ward off evil. Evil, whether it was the threat of pests or spoiling, would get confused and not come in. A lot of containers had a zigzag pattern."

My focus had fizzled, and it was time to go. Gilbertson had been a peach, and I thanked her for a remarkable tour. Walking to my car, I noticed a hand-lettered sign taped to a storefront window across from the museum. It was September, and the high school football season was in full swing. No doubt this sign infused the fear of thunder and Thor into the Xavier Saints, the next opponent of the Decorah Vikings: "Rose MAUL the Saints!"

Only in Decorah.

Everything that's creative in our Norwegian heritage takes patience. For children to learn patience with lefse making is great. I do sandbakkels, krumkake, lefse—all these cooking things as well as rosemaling, woodcarving, embroidery—it all takes patience.

–Janice Knudson Redford, 75, Cambridge, Wisconsin

DON'T FORGO
THE FLATBREAD ROLLERS

Even though your focus should be on lefse artifacts at Vesterheim, give yourself time to check out the narrow flatbread rolling tools—which, by the way, you can use to roll lefse. Such creativity with these kitchen tools!

In my Vesterheim tour, it struck me that some flatbread rollers looked like roller skate wheels on a stick. Some had Y-shaped metal handles that held wooden rollers. Three were ergonomically designed with a grooved roller set in a frame that was constructed with two side supports connected by two braces. A handle attached to the braces. Presumably, said Laurann Gilbertson, Vesterheim's chief curator, the flatbread/lefse maker could grip the handle with one hand and press on the frame with the other.

I was dumbfounded by two pieces, one a flatbread-rolling tool with a wooden handle. An iron holder with a twining ridge encased the handle. The hollow roller had 12 rows, each with 26 grooved teeth, and the roller was "possibly antelope horn," said the description.

Flatbread roller, 1870-1900.

The other striking specimen was not used for flatbread or lefse, but it was so cool I couldn't pass it up. It was a 14-inch-wide rolling cookie mold from Norway. Description: "Small rolling pin with double line grids dividing roller into squares, each containing a carved out plant or animal motif." One of the handles ended with a knob used to hang the pin. It was dated 1950 and found in Minneota, Minnesota.

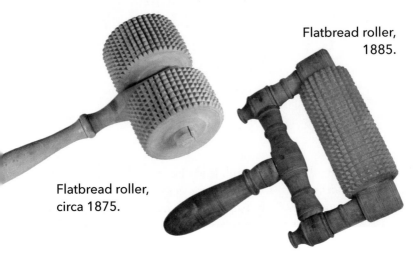

Flatbread roller, 1885.

Flatbread roller, circa 1875.

5
Cresco, Iowa

People are fascinated by lefse making.
We'll have folks from other cultures come by
when we're making lefse, and they'll talk about
foods in their culture. As we share ideas
and sample recipes, it's important to learn from
other people about their heritage.

—Louise Hanson, 66, Rochester, Minnesota

In *The Good Book of Lefse*, you'll find Cresco in "Genesis." Lefse baking, for all intents and purposes, begins here in Cresco at Bethany Housewares. You see, lefse newbies invariably make a significant purchase that supports the local economy of Cresco

Roxie Svoboda is president of Bethany Housewares, which produces about 10,000 lefse grills annually.

(pop. 3,879 in 2013). They may not know Cresco from Crisco at the time, but as they become lefse aficionados and make it to the promised land of proficiency, they learn to turn toward Cresco and bow to Bethany.

A lefse maker, like any artist creating a thing of beauty, relies heavily on tools and equipment. Bethany sells 53 items (at last count) of Scandinavian/Norwegian cookware. Most of these items are made at a variety of places, but the most critical piece of lefse-making equipment, the grill, is produced in Cresco.

Bethany makes all the lefse grills in the world. It has cornered the market. Will the Federal Trade Commission (FTC) drag Bethany into court to enforce antitrust laws? Nah. No company has stepped up to compete with Bethany, probably because the market is limited and tooling for the aluminum lefse grills is expensive. Since the 1950s these unique grills have been reliable and often prized in families. If the FTC were to come down on Bethany, lefse makers would rise up in protest and, brandishing their rolling pins, take it to the streets.

Why Cresco?

"We purchased Bethany Housewares from Bethany Fellowship Lutheran Seminary in Bloomington, Minnesota," said Roxie Svoboda, Bethany Housewares' president. "Bethany had, and still has, its publishing company. Bethany also made a pop-up camper and owned the housewares division where seminary students worked to make money for tuition. My dad, Paul Krysan, found their camper business interesting. He owned a CarQuest and a Radio Shack here, and he was always looking to bring new businesses to Cresco."

But Krysan passed on buying the camper business because manufacturing was too expensive for him and there was too much liability involved. A few years later, however, Bethany came back to Krysan about buying the housewares division. He did and moved Bethany Housewares to Cresco in 1988.

I asked Svoboda if her family had Scandinavian roots that swayed Krysan's decision to buy. "Nope, none," she said. "But Dad knew the Scandinavian influence was big here, 20 miles west of Decorah."

Injera, Anyone?

Svoboda said Bethany produces about 10,000 grills a year and has six full-time employees and one part-time worker. "The market has grown—probably four times—since we purchased the company," she said. "We pretty much cover the whole country. Minnesota is Scandinavian, of course, and we have pockets in the Dakotas, Wisconsin, and Iowa. Then we skip over to Scandinavian pockets in Montana, Washington, and Oregon."

Bethany sells nonstick grills to Ethiopian people living all over the nation, with clusters in Minnesota, Virginia, California, Washington state, and Washington, D.C. "Ethiopians use the grill to make one of their native breads, injera," said Svoboda. "Injera is made with teff flour. It is dense and looks like a tortilla, but thicker. Our injera business is pretty much year-round, whereas our lefse business is busy starting in the fall, when people begin thinking about Christmas."

Taking the Tour

Bethany's two-story, 10,500-square-foot plant looked to be the size of a small-town car dealership. Framed photos of lefse grill models, past and present, were on the walls in the front area where walk-in customers could check out Bethany's products and do business. There were few outside windows in the work area, but fluorescent lighting and a high ceiling made for pleasant working conditions. However, episodes of noise from grinding or drilling the aluminum grill plates were enough to stop all conversation.

As we began my tour of the plant, Svoboda explained that grills were cast at a St. Paul foundry, and the 735 Silverstone Heritage Grills with their nonstick Teflon finish were coated at Nordic Ware in Minneapolis. "We bring the grills in, tool them, sand them, and put them together," she said.

Svoboda added that Bethany workers also cut the interior rolling rods and assembled the Bethany maple rolling pins, put hinges on its stovetop krumkake bakers, and assembled and put finishing touches on its rosette makers. Off-site companies turned or cast all items. Similarly, a firm in Des Moines, Iowa,

While lefse grill models have changed, Bethany's market has grown four times since 1988.

provided square pastry boards that Bethany employees cut into circles and covered with pastry cloths. Each pastry cloth was screened at Bethany with red hash marks arranged in 10-, 12-, and 14-inch circles to help lefse makers roll rounds to a desired size.

We stopped in a brightly lit room with a big table. "We screen all our pastry cloths here," Svoboda said. "We buy fabric in 100-yard bolts and roll the fabric out on the table, 125 layers thick. We cut a circle through all the layers, and then a gal sews a drawstring into each pastry cloth. We also sew our aprons, hot pads, covers, and cozies."

Bethany used to make its own lefse sticks and wood handles for the grills. "We have the local Amish make our grill handles," Svoboda said. "And we import the finished sticks from China, still maintaining the quality we require."

We moved to a darker room where unfinished grill plates were neatly stacked waist high along one wall. Bethany developed a drilling machine that all at once creates holes in the grill for the handles, the plastic legs, and the aluminum guard around the electric probe control. After holes are drilled, Bethany employees sand each grill, sand again with fine sandpaper, and attach handles, legs, aluminum spacers between legs and grill, and the control guard. Finally, the electric probe control and the finished grill are packaged.

"We do all manufacturing of the components of our grills," Svoboda said. "On the press, we punch out the spacers and aluminum guards that go around the electric probe controls. And a machine drills holes in the wood handles, inserts pins used to connect handles to grill, and bends the pins, all at once in a three-step process."

Parting Tip

As the tour ended, I had one more question: "How long do Bethany grills last? After all, they retail for about $110 for the aluminum grill and $130 for the Teflon-coated grill."

"Oh, we've got grills out there that are 50 years old," said Svoboda. "It depends on how the grill is cared for, basically, and if it's used properly. What typically breaks down first is the electric control. As stated in the manual, don't run the grill for more than one and a half to two hours. The grill is OK to run for that long, but the control is plastic, and 500 degrees is hotter than most appliances go."

Svoboda said something next that I had never heard in all my years of making lefse. **TIP: "So if you alternate the controls, you'll have better luck making your grill last longer. Have two controls; we sell just the control separately. Put a different control in every hour, and let the other one cool off. We have people get together as a family and bake for eight hours. The grill is OK; it can handle it. It's the control that you should change every hour or so."**

Live and learn on the Lefse Trail.

We had many failures, but we had lots of fun trying to make lefse by ourselves. Barry's mom, Olga Bjornson Rosvold, came and helped us make a good batch of lefse, but she never used a recipe. It took a long time to do it by myself. It wasn't until I got a recipe from somebody else—that turned the tide. Then I got better and better at it, and now I make really good lefse. While others in the family try to make lefse, I'm still the Chief Lefse Maker. We went to the family reunion with Barry's mom, and she asked me to bring the lefse. I was quite thrilled, especially since I'm not Norwegian but British.

–Diane Rosvold, 69, Turner Valley, Alberta, Canada

Rick Naymark is known as the Gas Station Gastronomist.

THE GLORIES OF GAS STATIONS

Along the Lefse Trail you'll stop at many gas stations. Appreciate them. They are more than just places to pump gas, according to my friend Rick Naymark, also known as the Gas Station Gastronomist.

"Pumping gas is a small part of what gas stations do, probably a minor part of their revenue—maybe even a loss leader," says the Gastronomist. "They have all the things that make for a good retail experience. Easy access. Free parking. They're well lit, safe, welcoming, and clean with linoleum-type floors. There's little waiting in line. Efficiency—take care of your car and your body at the same time. They combine aspects of all sorts of stores—drug store, auto-parts store, grocery store, lottery outlet, soda fountain—all in one place. They're like a mini-mall but more convenient, and there's something happy about them.

"These are oases along the long highway of life where you can pause and be with other people. They're like a community bulletin board in real time. Gas stations aren't as segregated as other retail outlets. … Millionaires, poor people, middle class, they all go in gas stations. They're forced to look at each other, sometimes interact. Gas stations are the great equalizer.

"Sometimes in small towns on the Lefse Trail and elsewhere, gas stations *are* the local economy. They're the social hub and chief place of employment. They're just gas stations, but because they're *good* gas stations that are well signed on the freeway, they will attract other businesses. Maybe little restaurants, like a Subway, will open next to them. People will stop for gas and also have a quick lunch or dinner. The next step up is a motel that will co-locate. And so on. Gas stations are often the first step in economic development in a small town. There are lots of things to like about gas stations that have nothing to do with gas."

According to the Gas Station Gastronomist, food is a major attraction at the best stations. He says, "I can mix my beverage the way I like it, say Diet Coke and Cherry Coke together. At the coffee bar, I have a choice to dilute the brew or mix caffeinated with decaffeinated, and use sweeteners and creamers to my liking.

"I can pick the kind of hot dog I want, and it's essential that the condiment bar be clean. Relishes, chopped onions, sauerkraut in the good stations—all these options are for building that individualized dining experience. The price is usually much cheaper than a restaurant. … I can have all-beef patties, pizza, salads, and soup I can ladle into my own little paper cup.

"Believe it or not, one of the leading indicators of well-run gas stations is the condition of their bananas. There will be a wicker banana basket near the checkout. If those bananas are not ripe or are overripe, it says the rest of the food could be problematic."

Amen.

Imagine if you could pick up fresh lefse at a gas station. *That* would be worth stopping for!

Big Foot owner Glen McDowell holds
"the best chicken in Minnesota."

"BEST CHICKEN IN MINNESOTA"

The Gas Station Gastronomist, aka Rick Naymark, has presented his case for what constitutes the glorious gas-station
experience when traveling the Lefse Trail. The station that
would be Exhibit A in support of Rick's case has to be Big
Foot Gas & Grocery & Deli in Vining, Minnesota.

I pulled into Big Foot, at the crossroads of Minnesota
210 and County 40, shaken after having white-knuckled it
through a sprawling blizzard that had closed I-94 west of
Fargo, North Dakota. That evening I was to speak at the
Jul celebration of the Leif Erikson Sons of Norway at the
Vining Community Center. The event would feature lefse

and lutefisk, décor by Barbara and Chuck Olson, and music by Gloria Axelson. I was to stay overnight at the home of Ann and Tom Rasmussen, but as I collected myself before going into Big Foot, I wondered if the menacing wind and sideways snow would abate enough for me to get home the next day. Oh, where lefse leads us!

I entered the store and immediately, *blessedly*, felt what Rick says about all well-run gas stations: There's "something happy" about them. I was hailed by owner Glen McDowell, a big guy with a friendly face. We talked weather (what else?), and then I checked out the store. It had everything imaginable, local and otherwise, but my first interest was food.

"Are you interested in some broasted chicken?" asked Glen. I wasn't, but then he added, "It's the best chicken in Minnesota."

I was dubious. I studied the breading. It appeared light and nicely browned and crisp. I ordered one piece, a breast.

"What else can I help with?" asked Glen. When I said I could not find a salad to my liking, he said, "You just want some greens and tomatoes and onions and such? Maybe some cheddar cheese? I can toss together a salad for you right here."

Glen said he'd bring my plate to the seating area by the window. I went to the bathroom (very clean), bought a Coke, and sat at a table. Glen soon set the plate before me. "Enjoy."

I did. Immensely. Later, Glen told me he orders fresh Gold'n Plump chicken twice weekly, marinates it in his own creation, coats it in his own breading, and broasts it to "keep the chicken in its own juices."

Well, I'll tell you, right then, during the worst day of the winter, *that* was the best chicken in Minnesota.

6
Rushford, Minnesota

When I make lefse or rosettes with Grandma [Lisa Bishopp] and Great-Grandma [Linda Johnston], I get a lot of time with them and cherish every moment. I like hearing stories, and everybody has their own story. People older than you, they know a lot more and you can gain a lot from them.

—Alana Bishopp, 11, Eau Claire and Eleva, Wisconsin

I won't sugarcoat this: The Lefse Trail has a hubbub a-brewing. I'm talking about lefse-rolling machines.

One faction of lefse lovers sneers at lefse-rolling machines, claiming machine-made lefse is second-rate. Moreover, they say, rolling machines put human rollers out of work and threaten the lefse-making tradition: Why make it when you can buy it? "Grandma would roll over in her grave," they gripe, "if she knew machines were rolling lefse."

Another faction of lefse enthusiasts lauds lefse-rolling machines, claiming the machines are *saving* the lefse tradition. These ingenious machines, they say, evolved because lefse rolling is hard labor and human lefse makers who can roll a good round and hold up over a long career are becoming harder and harder to find. Besides, most machine-rolled lefse tastes fine, and there's nothing wrong with convenience. The reality is there are times when you want to make lefse, but you just can't swing it.

I pondered the debate as I drove on Minnesota Highway 43, which descends from Interstate 90 through wooded bluffs into Rushford, Minnesota (pop. 1,720 in 2013), a picturesque small town along the Root River. I wondered on which side of the hubbub my grandma Jennie Legwold would have come down. She made excellent lefse in her home in nearby Peterson, Minnesota, but passed before the age of lefse-rolling machines. Based on what I witnessed of her all-welcoming and nonjudgmental nature, she probably would have had no problem with anyone going the machine-rolled route. When her days were full raising my dad, Conrad Legwold, and four other children, she might have chosen that route as well—if the lefse were good.

After the Flood

In downtown Rushford I met Mark Johnson, 58, co-owner with Scott James, 58, of Norsland Lefse. On the Lefse Trail, Norsland is one of the four commercial lefse factories that have mechanized all or part of the lefse-rolling process. In researching my first book in 1992, I had been to Norsland to interview Merlin Hoiness, who founded the company in 1981 and sold it in 1987. I wanted the lowdown on the nine lefse-rolling machines Norsland had used since the mid-1980s. Norsland had been forced to move to its current location after a flood on August 18, 2007, washed out the lefse factory and store.

If I were a Rushford resident, Norsland's 9,000-square-foot digs would be a place I could spend a lot of my day. I'd rise early and

Norsland Lefse's Mark Johnson says business has grown during the past 20 years, thanks to these nine lefse-rolling machines.

run or bike on the Root River State Trail and then reward myself at Norsland's bakery. Gee, what would I have? Vanilla long john rolls are my weakness, but it would be hard to pass on the lefse.

Treat in hand, I'd walk a few paces, find a table in Norsland's coffee shop, and write for a while over a cup of Earl Grey tea. After pounding out one impressive passage after another, I'd find further inspiration by enjoying brunch that included a lefse wrap of scrambled eggs, sausage, hash browns, and cheese drizzled with hollandaise sauce.

Settling into the coffee shop's friendly atmosphere, I'd linger and write a bit longer. Then I'd stretch my legs and walk down a hall to Norsland's gift shop, where I'd find my books along with other literary treasures. I'd also find Ekte Geitost goat cheese, Budz potato pancakes, Thorvald's Cream of Lutefisk Soup mugs, gloog drink mix, lingonberry syrup, almond-flavored kringla, Keep Calm and Eat Lefse T-shirts, Ole and Lena habanero salsa (yumpin' yiminy!), Minnesota wild rice, Viking horn helmets (so flattering!), Uffda golf balls, Proud to Be a Lil' Norskie teddy bears, Spring Grove soda pop, and lots of lefse-making gear.

01234567890123456789012345678901234567890

How's Business?

Johnson and I sat a spell in his office, and I commented that the combination of the gift shop, coffee shop, bakery, and lefse plant made Norsland unique among all other lefse factories on the Lefse Trail.

"Our business has grown every year for the last 20 years," he said. "Last year was our best year ever, and I don't think we've hit the top." He added that 75 percent of Norsland's sales are in the last quarter of the year, but revenue from the bakery, coffee shop, and gift shop help sustain the business in the first three quarters.

"Is it difficult finding workers?" I asked. Norsland employs 20 to 25 people, the equivalent of 10 to 12 full-time employees.

"We've been pretty lucky," he said. "Most people working here live in town and have some kind of a Scandinavian background or connection. They don't really want to be pushed. They like their summer off and the flexibility this type of business offers. But don't get me wrong, labor is always one of the bigger cost issues of any business."

Marveling at Machines

The time had come to see Norsland's featured attraction. Johnson led me to the lefse-production room, a pleasant workspace with five windows to the gift shop and six to the outside. The lefse-rolling machines—mesmerizing contraptions that invariably capture the curiosity of gift-shop customers—rested in a row, like a bank of brawny R2-D2s, ready to roll at the flip of a switch.

Years ago Hoiness ordered the custom-made machines from a local manufacturer (see "Humble Beginnings," page 61). "These machines are the original nine, and the only nine ever made," Johnson said. "They're 30-plus years old, and we really haven't adapted or changed them a bit. We've repaired them many times. There are lots of moving parts, and all these machines went through the flood. We had to strip them down and replace motors. The thing is, you don't call up the lefse-rolling machine repair shop and order a part; you have to make one. Some issues we are able to take care of: The machines are all chains, belts, pulleys, brackets, and sheet metal. But if we can't fix them, we take them to Connaughty Sales, a welding shop in Rushford, where a welder makes a new piece."

Considering the millions of back-and-forth passes those machine rollers have made over the decades, I was amazed the original nine were still in use and not in a museum. "If those machines were developed today—and we're thinking about making a new model someday—new technology and switches and such would make them a lot smoother, quieter, and more efficient. How much would it cost? It would take $10,000 per machine just to get the ball rolling.

"Many people—from churches or people who want to do this on their own—have asked, 'Can I buy one? Where do I get them?' A guy from Norway emailed me and called a couple of times. He was starting a little business and wanted to know where to get one. Well, you can't. He wanted me to make one for him. I'm not up for tackling that [manufacturing and selling lefse-rolling machines]. But if someone wants to make one, go ahead. Take a picture of it. Get into the lefse-making business too; I don't care."

How They Roll

Johnson showed me how Norsland makes 750,000 rounds of lefse a year. First, whole russet potatoes are dumped into a Hobart peeler, a machine that rubs off the skins. Peeled potatoes go into a cooker that holds 500 pounds of potatoes. Cooked spuds are stuffed into a meat grinder that squeezes the potatoes through a ricing screen. A Hobart mixer blends measured amounts of riced potatoes, soybean oil, and salt—no dairy or preservatives—to make the dough.

A worker shapes the dough into a 3-inch-thick rectangle, roughly 2 feet by 3 feet. This mass is fed through a roller that flattens the dough to an approximate 2-inch thickness. A worker presses into the dough a cutter that punches out a dozen 3-inch-by-3-inch squares, each weighing about ¼ pound. The squares are fed into another roller that spits ⅜-inch-thick, unfinished rounds onto a conveyor belt, where a worker presses a 9-inch circular cutter onto the unfinished rounds. This produces dough disks that are ready for showtime on the lefse-rolling machines.

The machine's 20-inch plywood rolling board is covered with a linen pastry cloth.

The rolling pin is weighted to increase rolling efficiency.

Using a lefse stick, a worker transfers the dough disks from the conveyor belt to the machine's 20-inch plywood rolling board. A linen pastry cloth covers the board and is secured by a huge worm-drive duct clamp. The worker dusts the dough and rolling pin with flour, flips a switch, and rolling begins.

To prevent sticking, a compression sock, secured with a rubber band at each end, covers the oak or maple grooved rolling pin. An axle goes through the pin. At each end, a steel oval the size of a hockey puck adds weight to increase rolling efficiency. Each end of the axle rides in a U-shaped steel fork that moves in a track and is secured to a chain. The main drive motor moves the chains on both sides of the pin, making the pin go back and forth, back and forth, back and forth.

Here is a look "under the hood" of a Norsland lefse-rolling machine. With repairs, these machines have held up well since 1984.

"The unique part is you still want a round piece, right?" said Johnson. "I mean, lefse is round! Well, if I put a piece of dough on that board, the roller's going to move back and forth and make the dough go oblong—unless that board rotates. So, a small motor in the machine has the proper timing to keep turning that board an eighth of a turn to a quarter of a turn after each pass."

I asked why the rolling pin rises at the end of each pass. "See how the track ramps up here and here?" Johnson said, pointing to each end of the track. "Those ramps cause the roller to lift slightly, and the lifting allows the board to rotate freely. So, the roller goes across, lifts, and the board pivots. Roller goes across, lifts, board pivots. And on and on."

Brilliant!

The roller requires about 16 passes to make a 15- to 16-inch round. When a round is rolled out, the worker flips the off switch. With a lefse stick, the worker lifts the lefse onto a long gas grill that burns at 550 degrees. Two or three cooks use lefse sticks to flip and tend the rounds. When a round is done, it goes to a 50-foot conveyor belt that slowly moves past fans stationed at several points along the length of the room.

After the round is cool, another worker brushes off excess flour and folds the lefse so that two rounds fit into one plastic package. Food-grade nitrogen gas is blown into the bag to extend the lefse's shelf life and provide a protective cushion of air. Finally, a Hobart heat sealer seals two bags at once.

Norsland sells nationwide, shipping orders of 3, 6, 12, and 24 packages. By the way, rounds that are less than perfect are sold as seconds, and rounds that are torn or burned are fried and become Uffda chips. "They're like tortilla chips with a really good seasoning of salt and savory spices or cinnamon and sugar," said Johnson.

About That Hubbub?

It had been a fascinating tour, and now a Norsland lefse wrap of turkey, cheese, lettuce, tomato, red onion, and chipotle mayo was calling my name. But I had one last question about the lefse-rolling machine hubbub. Were the Norsland machines threatening or saving the lefse-making tradition?

Johnson smiled. "You have to go back to when Merlin started," he explained. "Store-bought stuff wasn't quite as important, meaning Grandma made the lefse. Mom made the lefse. They were homemakers. That was what they did. Well, guess what? Times have changed, and 'grandma' is not here anymore, if you know what I mean. Not like grandmas and moms were there in Merlin's day. Today they say, 'For goodness sakes, I'm not going to make lefse—I don't have time—but I'm still going to carry on the tradition.' So who are we at Norsland Lefse? We're Grandma. We're Mom. We're filling that void.

"And then there are the church dinners. The ladies used to make lefse for these dinners, and they'd have a big, beautiful day of it. But those ladies, at least at many churches, aren't there anymore. Organizers say, 'I can't get enough help to make the lefse, but I still want to have a lutefisk dinner.' So Norsland Lefse fills that gap.

"Do I worry the lefse-making tradition is going to die? No, I don't know. There are still a lot of people who do it. I sell lots of lefse-starter kits [grill, lefse stick, lefse rolling pin, pastry cloth and board set, ricer, and recipe book]. You want to make it? Go for it. I want your kids to learn how to make it. It's just that we live in a fast-paced time, and husbands and wives are both working. Even if families buy from us, they're still getting their kids involved in these traditions."

I think we should call it practicing lefse instead of making lefse. I tell my kids when they're practicing music that they're practicing, not perfecting, music. I think there's something about the patience you learn with lefse. You look at it and say, "OK, I messed up. So what did I do wrong, and how can I change that next time?" You have to be patient.

—Kristin Klinefelter, 40, Grand Rapids, Minnesota

HUMBLE BEGINNINGS

Merlin Hoiness was a must interview when I was researching *The Last Word on Lefse*. After all, he was known as Mr. Lefse because he had written a book called *91 Ways to Serve Lefse*, which sold more than 40,000 copies before he died in 2013 at age 96. He and his wife, Zola, also did lefse-rolling shows throughout the region.

In 1992 over lunch at the Mill Street Inn in Rushford, Hoiness told me he had been in the grocery business his whole life and "could never keep the people satisfied when it came to lefse."

His lefse sources were women in town and on local farms. "I was actually bootlegging lefse, you see," he said. "These ladies weren't checked out by the public health inspector. He'd come into the store and ask who made my lefse. Then he'd have to take it off the shelf and throw it in the garbage."

To stop such wrongful waste, in 1981 Hoiness started Norsland Kitchens, which eventually became Norsland Lefse. The business grew, but the problem of meeting the lefse demand persisted. Thinking automation was the answer, Hoiness joined forces with Carroll Bakken and Al Spande to create a hand-operated lefse-rolling machine prototype. In 1984 they showed it to Jim Humble of Humble Manufacturing in Rushford, which specialized in wood-burning stoves and furnaces. Could he create a lefse-rolling machine?

Humble, who had retired the year before and had a life-long passion for building cars, designed and manufactured a model. He used surplus computer motors purchased for $10 each from IBM in Rochester, Minnesota. "I'm sure it took a lot of trial and error with different patterns to come up with a machine that could apply the right pressure with the roller and get everything just so," said Mark Johnson, Norsland's current owner.

Humble got everything just so and then completed the project of building the nine lefse-rolling machines that have been in use since and have earned Norsland a certain degree of notoriety on the Lefse Trail. Humble died in 2011 at age 91.

Jim Humble invented Norsland's lefse-rolling machines.

7
St. Paul, Minnesota

The only way you can sustain interest in a family lefse fest is to not subscribe to perfectionism. When you get into the perfect roll, then you intimidate. Sometimes when you're eating, you'll know that this is whoever's lefse, right? So what? Reeling back that ugly head of perfectionism has helped.

—Roxanne Hart, 62, St. Paul

The Lefse Trail not only can move you forward to one lefse refuge after another, but it can also take you back in time. So it seems at Northwest Casting, Inc. When touring this 35,000-square-foot St. Paul foundry, it's as if you've stepped back into the early days of the Industrial Revolution.

"Wait, Northwest Casting is a *foundry*?" you may ask. "Are we still on the Lefse Trail?"

Indeed, we are. Northwest Casting is the lefse grill's square one. Bethany Housewares produces lefse grills made of aluminum. Northwest Casting first inserts a circular electrical heating element into a lefse-grill mold and then pours melted aluminum into the mold. When the aluminum cools and solidifies around the heating element, it becomes a casting. Northwest Casting is the sole manufacturer of these lefse-grill castings that Bethany workers sand, finish, and ship all over the world.

Moeller Made

Lefse is such a happy food, but grill manufacturing in a foundry seems to be an unsmiling business. The deafening noise, ominous smoke, acrid smells, 1,200-degree heat, glowing cauldrons, hellish ovens, brooding ventilation hoods, frantic fans, thick gloves, thick boots, and quicksilver flash of menacing, molten aluminum give this place the appearance of a volcano's throat. This is the stuff of Dickens.

Into this Northwest Casting scene limped a man Hollywood could cast as Joe Gargery, the village blacksmith and Pip's brother-in-law in *Great Expectations.* Bill Moeller, 62, manager of molding operations, had what you could imagine to be Joe's look, strength, patience, and sense of humor. He's the guy you want making the most important piece of lefse equipment you'll own.

Moeller gave me a tour of the foundry's spacious, two-stories-high work area. It was dark but sufficiently lit by overhead lamps and dozens of clouded 3-by-6-foot windows evenly spaced on the outside walls. Despite my eye and ear protection, too many of Moeller's explanations were barely audible because of piercing production noises. But during quiet breaks, Moeller could hold forth. He picked up a Bethany Housewares lefse grill and said, "This is an excellent product that's been around a long time. The die maker really did a good job with the die for that grill."

Moeller said a die is a device for cutting or molding metal into a particular shape. In this case the shape is of a lefse grill

Bill Moeller stands next to a casting oven. He says the lefse grill is a difficult casting because it is thin and contains a heating element.

with holes for the grill's legs, handles, and heating element. He said a tool-and-die maker in Lakeville, Minnesota, created all Northwest Casting dies.

"I think we're on the third die for the lefse grill, and the last die cost about $20,000," said Moeller. "Dies aren't cheap, but they last a long time. It's nothing for a die to last 100,000 castings. If you get 50,000 to 60,000 out of it, that's still pretty good. We're known for our dies lasting a long time. We keep up maintenance, watch our temperatures close, and take good care of them. You hate to have to tell a customer, 'Hey, you gotta spend 20 grand.' That goes over really well! Bethany owns that lefse grill die. Roxie [Svoboda, Bethany Housewares' president] is a very good customer."

Why Not China?

We moved to shelves holding about 20 dies used to make Northwest Casting's products. In addition to lefse grills, Northwest Casting manufactures such products as golf ball washers, golf distance markers, wenches, hydraulic parts for manhole covers on railroad cars, soup warmers for gas stations, and chair backs for the U.S. Navy. This family-owned jobbing foundry was established in 1937. When Moeller started working here in 1974, there were 40 employees; now there are 13.

It's a familiar story, said Moeller: "So much stuff is made overseas now. The first job we lost overseas was a part the customer said China would do for less cost. They'd make the tooling, make the parts, machine them, ship them, drop them off at the customer's dock—in other words they could do the job for basically a third of our cost. How can you compete with that?"

"Good question," I said. "So why doesn't Bethany Housewares go to China for the lefse grills?"

"The quantity is not that high," Moeller said. "China comes in play with a large quantity. Let's say you order 5,000. China wants you to order 20,000 at a pop; otherwise, they don't make it. Also, China is far away, and if there are problems with that casting, it's your tough luck. We go after customers they can't go after, small-run customers. That's the only way we can make some bucks. We've quoted high-quantity jobs, but the problem is, yeah, you can get the job and stick $100,000 into new tooling and other things to handle the castings. Then two years later, they say, 'See ya later. Your casting was two cents higher than the other guy's.'"

Lefse Grill: Tough Casting

Production noise returned, and we moseyed on. We stopped where lefse grills were made and waited for the decibel level to drop. We leaned against a cauldron, about 4 feet tall and 5 feet wide, with a concrete wall as thick as the diameter of a lefse grill. On the wall were ingots (bars) of aluminum, grill castings, an unused copper heating element, and another element turned gray after a worker recovered it from a defective casting.

When the noise abated, Moeller pointed to the defective casting. "This is a very tough casting," he said. "It's tough because of how thin it is. Aluminum is pushed under pressure [3,500 pounds per square inch] into a die in order to get the grill thin and strong.

Still, if you don't cast it right, a grill that thin can sag when heated up. Also, it's tough because we cast a heating element in it. The grill is for food so Roxie wants it perfectly clean. That's pretty hard to get consistently with aluminum. Aluminum oxidizes so fast, and oxidation is junk in metal. Think of it as rust, except the oxidation is with aluminum and not iron.

"We constantly use cleaners to draw out that oxidation. We use filters that remove the dross [impurities floating on or dispersed in molten metal]. Plus, heated aluminum becomes gassy with hydrogen. If you don't pull that gas out, the casting may look fine on the outside, but on the inside it would look like a sponge because of the gas. To minimize the gas, we keep our temperature down and run another gas, argon, through the metal. Argon attaches to the hydrogen and lifts it out."

We headed out of the workspace and into a quiet, carpeted conference room. It was lunchtime, and the tour was over. Most other stops on the Lefse Trail conclude with lefse consumption, but not this one. It was a foundry, after all.

I thanked Moeller and asked if he made lefse. "No," he said, "but I use the lefse grill for pancakes and French toast. Nothing can touch that grill as far as quality and thickness go. It ain't cheap—like $100 or so—but it's five times the grill as anything else."

Mom and Dad gave a lefse grill as a wedding present. I said, "Heavens, I need to start doing this!" I always used to help Mom turn lefse. She did the mixing and rolling. Sometimes Dad would help, but she'd get mad at him because he liked the lefse darker than she did. He liked it almost burned. So she would try to train the kids instead of Dad training us.

—Janet (Larson) Spracklin, 60, Sidney, Montana

Reeves Cary, right, once asked his dad, Kermit Cary, why lefse has brown spots. Dad couldn't resist telling a fib.

LEFSE, SNOOSE, AND A "RAILROAD TO HELL"

Snoose (snuff, or chewing tobacco), so they say, stimulates the soul and shortens long hours of hard labor. Railroad contractor Michael J. Heney so believed in the power of snoose that when building the White Pass & Yukon Route Railroad over the rugged Coast Mountains in 1898, he said, "Give me enough dynamite and snoose, and I'll build a railroad to hell." This snoose power applies to those whose labor is making lefse. Reeves Cary grew up in Twin Valley, Minnesota, population 800. "This Scandinavian town was so small you could drive in, but you'd have to back out," said Reeves, who lives in Minneapolis. When Reeves was 5 years old, he questioned his father, Kermit Cary, about how lefse got brown spots. "Dad said lefse makers chewed snoose," recalled Reeves. "They'd spit the juice, but they'd dribble. The brown spots were from their dribbles. Well, *that* turned me off, I'll tell you. I didn't eat lefse for several years."

8
Osakis, Minnesota

I think the only time I saw my grandmother Mari Haugen smile was when she offered lefse.

–Cordell Keith Haugen, 76, Nuuanu Valley, Hawaii

If you had to personify lefse, you might say it is confident but shy. Lefse knows it is good, the belle of the ball at any Scandinavian food event. But it's also reluctant to say so, which isn't surprising considering it is made by Scandinavians, who are stereotyped as shy. What's the old joke? When you talk with Scandinavians, how do you separate extroverts from introverts? The extroverts look at *your* shoes.

Given this shyness, Scandinavians are probably blown away by a billboard located on Interstate 94 in northern Minnesota. It's 14 feet high and 48 feet wide—672 square feet of red-and-blue signage that bears resemblance to the flag of Norway. It has these words, in yellow:

JACOBS LEFSE BAKERI & GIFTS
Just ahead—Exit 114 Osakis

It's pretty dang difficult not to check this out. So Osakis (pop. 1,720 in 2013), about 12 miles east of Alexandria, is the next stop on the Lefse Trail.

On a Monday afternoon in November, I entered the 2,886-square-foot facility through a bright red door. The gift shop was stocked with books, lefse-making equipment, Scandinavian novelty items, framed words-of-inspiration wall hangings, glass vases, lingonberry preserves, mustards, and on and on. Atop a blue counter were trays of almond cakes and white baskets of Swedish coconut cookies, almond biscotti, caramel peanut popcorn, and almond cookies, all guaranteed to generate involuntary groans of pleasure once they pass your lips. On the other side of the paneled wall behind the counter was the lefse-production area.

Bonnie Jacobs, 64, the owner, stood behind the counter. She has nine mostly part-time employees who make lefse year-round. Two more join in rush times. During the holiday season, they make 1,100 to 1,200 rounds daily from 5 a.m. to 10 a.m. In the afternoon, as Bonnie and office manager Joanne Ranum

You can't miss this billboard while driving Interstate 94 in central Minnesota.

During the holiday season, Jacobs makes 1,100 to 1,200 lefse rounds daily from 5 a.m. to 10 a.m.

were filling orders and prepping for the next day, I asked about the billboard.

"For three to four years, I tried all sorts of advertising to get people off the interstate," Bonnie said. "I even advertised on WCCO radio [in Minneapolis]. Ten years ago I put up the billboard by Sauk Centre [for those heading west], and then I added one coming from Fargo [for those heading east]. They're expensive, but I get business off of them. They're my best form of advertising, the billboards and doing about 35 trade shows a year."

Started With Pastry Board

My first encounter with the Jacobs family was while researching *The Last Word on Lefse*. I had interviewed Dennis Jacobs, Bonnie's brother, who was running the House of Jacobs in Spicer, Minnesota, with shops in nearby Willmar and New London. In 1972, according to the company history, their mother, Bernice Jacobs, struggled with lefse sticking to the counter as she rolled. John Jacobs, her husband, came up with the solution by making a 23½-inch round pastry board with a cotton-polyester cover. Word got out about this pastry board and cover—not to mention Bernice's lefse—and soon Dennis had developed a business of selling lefse and related products.

The Osakis store opened in 2000. Dennis retired in 2013, and Bonnie's running the show now. "The sad part is when I close or sell or whatever, there will be no one in the Jacobs family doing the business," said Bonnie. "I'm the last one who's still working. My children have other careers and are not attracted to living in a small town and working 10 to 12 hours a day, seven days a week. And I'm way too fussy to have someone else come in and run it."

Bonnie said production was busier than ever, and the company continues to grow. "The challenge is not having to shut down the website in the middle of December, which we've done because we cannot keep up with orders," she said. "It's been a few years since we've been able to go right through December without limiting wholesale orders so we can keep up with the retail business. We could hire more, but I don't know how many more hours I want to be here. It's hard to know which way to go with it. But I think we're going to do pretty well this year. Don't you, Joanne?"

Seasonal Insanity

"Every year we say we're not going to shut down the website early, but this year we *are,*" Joanne said.

"Oh, yeah, we have orders hanging all over the place," Bonnie added. "We have two phone lines, and between the phones ringing with orders and us pulling orders off the computer, it's chaotic. We're also set up at the mall in Alexandria, so I have someone working that. How do we handle it? We all stress out."

"Was it last year I was rationing lefse on Christmas Eve?" asked Joanne. "We had very few packages left, and I would put most of them in the fridge in back so customers couldn't take like 10 packages from the fridge in the gift shop. That's what they started doing in the morning, coming in and grabbing all the lefse."

"They came in off the interstate," said Bonnie. "That's why I got those two big signs there."

"I just put a limited number of packages in the gift-shop fridge, and customers would say, 'Oh, there's four packages in here. Is that it?'" said Joanne. "And somebody *else* would come in, and I'd say 'Don't fight over it.' Then they'd share."

I asked if they were ever concerned that this shortage would require a call to security. "It's December 24, and they all need lefse," said Joanne, laughing, "so they don't dare cause trouble. I don't mind the stress as long as I can stay organized and on top of it. It's only for like two months, and it's certainly better than not being busy."

Turning Down Lefse?!

Price did not seem to be a factor in how busy the company was. Bonnie said she sold lefse wholesale to churches at $1.10 a round, stores and other wholesale groups at $1.30 a round, and directly to customers at $2.10 a round.

"Wholesale people try to find cheaper lefse that sells for 50 cents a round. But then it's not any good, so they come back to us," Bonnie said. "They find out it's just better to pay the price and have good lefse. Ours is better. I'm not kidding. Isn't it, Joanne?"

"It's true," said Joanne. "Would you like a roll-up?"

"We'll give you some!" Bonnie said to me.

Normally, I'm always down for lefse. But I thought I would have some fun, so with as much of a straight face as I could manage, I said, "You couldn't *force* me to eat lefse."

They were stunned, almost as if I had told them anthropologists had just discovered the origins of lefse were Polish, not Norwegian. "What?" screeched Joanne. "Then get out of here!"

The stakes (free lefse) were too high, so I decided to smile and drop the pretense. "No, I love lefse."

"Would you like a roll-up?" Joanne repeated.

Some years Jacobs has to ration lefse on Christmas Eve.

"Sure!"

"What would you like on it?"

"Butter, sugar, and cinnamon."

Just like that, I had a warmed roll-up in my hand and took a bite. It was delicious lefse, the perfect afternoon pick-me-up. As I ate the rest of the round, I listened to Bonnie talk about the crazed lefse market at Christmastime. "When we're shipping out of the five-state area, customers have to pay air price. So they're paying $23 for four packages of our lefse, and on top of that they pay $40 to $50 to get it there in two days. And it's all day long we take those orders! So customers don't care when it comes to getting lefse."

Bonnie Jacobs has two rounds grilling while she rolls a third.

No Whining

It was time to tour. After we walked through the swinging doors to the production area, what first grabbed my attention was a sign that no doubt generated more humor than income: "THERE WILL BE A $5.00 CHARGE FOR WHINING." I made a point not to whine as I asked questions about producing large amounts of lefse year-round.

Four grills dominated the room. Each gas grill, set at 500 degrees, comfortably holds two rounds that are rolled large enough so they cook down to 14 inches in diameter. Next to each grill is a steel table with a round, covered pastry board.

Each roller—Bonnie is one—also grills. Each skilled worker has two rounds grilling while she rolls a third. The round starts as a one-third-cup patty of dough, and each round is flipped once during rolling. The rolled-out round hisses on the grill for 11 to 13 seconds on side A, and just 7 seconds on side B. This quick cooking helps keep the lefse moist. Finished rounds go to a tray that holds 25, and full trays are covered and go to a rack where the rounds cool for two hours to room temperature. The rounds are then packaged and rolled to a refrigerator for overnight cooling. The next day, packages are stored in freezers.

"Our lefse freezes really well," said Bonnie. "A lot of it is because of the potatoes. We use a dry potato mix. We don't use potato flakes. Our potato mix is granulated white potatoes, flour, margarine, sugar, salt, and milk products. We started using the mix in Willmar to save on labor, and we've stayed with it for 38 years. Lefse made with real potatoes sometimes has a hard time with freezing; the variable moisture in the potatoes can mean the lefse is too wet, and the rounds can stick together when you freeze and then thaw them."

Two Lefse Tips

I asked Bonnie if family lefse making has a solid future. She had concerns that the "younger kids aren't keeping up," she said, "but I know there are still a lot of people who make it. We make and sell pastry boards, and we still sell replacement covers. So families are making it. People may think lefse making's dying out, but a lot of homes still make it."

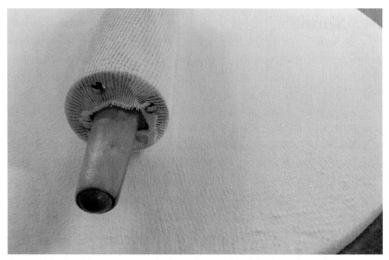

Bonnie's tip: Secure your lefse-pin sock with thumbtacks.

To help people make good lefse, Bonnie offered two tips.

If you are annoyed when the sock on your lefse rolling pin slips and exposes one end of the wood roller, Bonnie has this **TIP:** "**Secure the sock with thumbtacks on the ends of the roller. You don't want to take time to adjust the sock, so if you tack the ends, it won't slide.**"

If you are cursed with the drive to make a perfectly round lefse, Bonnie suggests this **TIP:** "**It starts with the dough. If it's not mixed enough, the edges will crack when you roll. Never cut the edges. Are you kidding? They aren't all going to be perfect. They're hand rolled, so some will be jaggy. Here's my best advice on trying to make perfectly round lefse: Do it more than once a year.**"

This is a lofty goal for me, to really get as good as I can at making lefse. I enjoy it, I really do. You can make a lot of jokes about Norwegians and Ole and Lena things and all of the stuff that

Norwegians are known for, but I came from a German-Scottish family and wanted to be close to the Norwegian tradition. Rolling lefse has helped. Furthermore, our three daughters ... have learned how to roll, and their husbands have learned. None of them are as good as their dad/ father-in-law, but they're trying.

—Bill Wilson, 69, Scotts Mills, Oregon

HOW TO SAY *OSAKIS*

Before stopping at Jacobs Lefse Bakeri & Gifts in Osakis, take a moment to learn how to say *Osakis*. I was pronouncing *Osakis* all sorts of ways, and for some reason the proper pronunciation wasn't sticking in my noggin. To avoid embarrassment, I simply stopped *saying* it.

You say *oh-SAY-kiss*,
And I say *oh-SAH-keys*.
Perhaps it's *OH-say-kiss*,
Or maybe *oh-sah-KEYS*?
oh-SAY-kiss?
oh-SAH-keys?
say kiss or sah keys?
Let's call the whole thing off!

Don't call the whole thing off when you visit this lefse shop. *Osakis* is such a pretty word—and a pretty town on the southwest shore of Lake Osakis. So when *say*ing Osakis, just *say* it this way: *oh-SAY-kiss!*

9
Starbuck, Minnesota

It's lefse appreciation, and as you get older it turns into wisdom. I've been an appreciator since my first bite at age 2. My grandma Tora Tviberg Norheim always handed each kid two lefse. "One for each hand, to keep you busy," she'd say. It's time to learn from Grandma.

—Sally Norheim Dwyer, 62, Petersburg, Alaska

People who know the lore of lefse will find it a no-brainer that Starbuck is on the Lefse Trail. Inhabitants of this small town (pop. 1,274 in 2013) on the western shore of Lake Minnewaska modestly downplay lefse's role in Starbuck's survival and vitality. But the World's Largest Lefse put this town on the map and is keeping

Starbuck vibrant. Admittedly, I'm looking through lefse lenses here and reaching a bit, but that's my story and I'm sticking to it.

You see, the first thing that catches your eye as you drive into town on North Main Street are 5-foot-tall blue banners placed proudly and high on every red lamppost. Each banner has rosemaling above the words *Home of ... World's Largest Lefse.* Starbuck also boasts a 10-foot-wide concrete-and-pebble circle with a commemorative brass plate in the center. It marks the spot near the Starbuck Depot where this historic lefse-making event occurred on July 1, 1983. Now, if that's not the national monument to lefse, I don't know what is.

Humans are lured to large things like blue whales, giant sequoias, African elephants—and a 9-foot 8-inch, 70-pound lefse. This big lefse rollout was the featured event of Starbuck's first Heritage Days, a celebration of the town's centennial. The success of Heritage Days made it an annual festival that's still

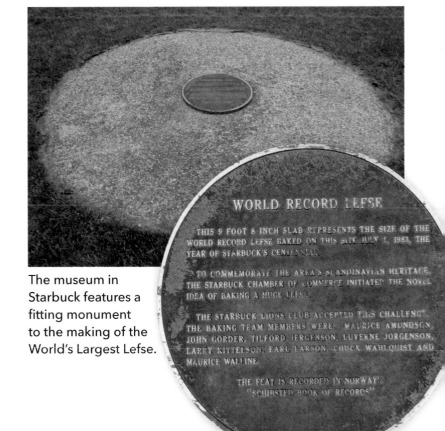

The museum in Starbuck features a fitting monument to the making of the World's Largest Lefse.

WORLD RECORD LEFSE

THIS 9 FOOT 8 INCH SLAB REPRESENTS THE SIZE OF THE WORLD RECORD LEFSE BAKED ON THIS SITE JULY 1, 1983, THE YEAR OF STARBUCK'S CENTENNIAL.

TO COMMEMORATE THE AREA'S SCANDINAVIAN HERITAGE, THE STARBUCK CHAMBER OF COMMERCE INITIATED THE NOVEL IDEA OF BAKING A HUGE LEFSE.

THE STARBUCK LIONS CLUB ACCEPTED THIS CHALLENGE. THE BAKING TEAM MEMBERS WERE: MAURICE AMUNDSON, JOHN GORDER, TILFORD JERGENSON, LUVERNE JORGENSON, LARRY KITTELSON, EARL LARSON, CHUCK WAHLQUIST AND MAURICE WALLINE.

THE FEAT IS RECORDED IN NORWAY'S "SCHIBSTED BOOK OF RECORDS"

A kiddie parade adds to the fun of Heritage Days in Starbuck.

Master lefse makers teach the young to roll at Lefse Dagen.

going strong today, with a parade, festival royalty, style show, tea party, dance, Miss Minnewaska pageant, fun run, golf tournament, crafts, games, pancake breakfast, food booths, and fireworks.

Since 1987 Starbuck has also celebrated Lefse Dagen, an annual mid-May fete that honors the World's Largest Lefse. Activities for the 2017 Lefse Dagen include music ("Tennessee Ernie Fjord" and Shari Opdahl and the Glacial Hills Elementary singers), Scandinavian food (roll-your-own lefse, rommegrot, fruit soup), crafts sales, and lefse-making demonstrations by the Pederson Holy Rollers. Lefse Dagen is sponsored by the Starbuck Depot Society and the Starbuck Study Club. In 2006 the Depot Society commissioned the creation of a wall-wide collage of photos of the rolling and grilling of the World's Largest Lefse and unveiled it to the public during Lefse Dagen.

Big Lefse, Big Impact

"The World's Largest Lefse has turned the depot into the focal point of Starbuck," said Jeannie Pladsen, depot treasurer. "Without that record lefse, people from out of town would not come this far down into town and have picnics. The depot building would not exist, and it would not be a place for people to gather and do events.

"After the record was set, we brought a small, old country schoolhouse to the depot area. People come to the schoolhouse and check out all the memorabilia from the high school that was here at the time. We've started Thursday Night on the Town here at the depot. Organizations sign up for a date in June through the end of August, and they serve a

Jeannie Pladsen says the world-record lefse draws travelers into downtown Starbuck.

In Starbuck the museum shows the giant tools used to make the World's Largest Lefse.

dinner to the community. We also have a farmers market here. And it's the social thing for the community to do, to come here and sit and visit and listen to piano, accordion, and guitar music and have sing-alongs. And then there's Eple Tiden, which is Norwegian for Apple Time. It's a market-day celebration held here and features apples, pumpkins, and other garden produce brought to Starbuck by various vendors."

In sum, big lefse is a big deal in Starbuck, all because of what began as a wacky idea.

Beyond the city limits, nothing has tickled the fancy of lefse aficionados more and generated more sustained media coverage in Lefse Land than the making of the World's Largest Lefse.

No Dough, No Show

In 1992 I interviewed six Lions Club members who made up most of the team that created the World's Largest Lefse. I devoted an entire chapter in *The Last Word on Lefse* to their failures and false starts—and one huge success. The interview took place at what was then Gordy's Café. It was a funny and fascinating morning as these representatives of the "Boys of Starbuck" told their tall-but-true tale.

Ever since that day, I had been keen to talk with Larry Kittelson, who was not at the 1992 gathering at Gordy's. Larry is owner of the Pastry Shoppe and the baker who was the linchpin of this loony lefse project. The invention of the grill, the gathering of ridiculous amounts of ingredients for the dough, the crafting of the 12-foot-long rolling pin, the transformation of a hayrack into a rolling surface—all of these were crucial to the project's success. Larry made the dough—and then reformulated it at the 11th hour when a trial run had failed. Larry was key because, as all lefse makers know, if you don't have the dough, there ain't no show.

I was nervous when I called Larry. I didn't know if he would remember *The Last Word on Lefse,* and I didn't know how the book had been received in Starbuck. Maybe the town hated it, and Larry would blow me off. He didn't answer my call, so I left a voicemail message.

He called back the next day, and I explained that I would like him to lead a team that re-created the World's Largest Lefse, maybe as a part of Lefse Dagen or Heritage Days. I stressed that I didn't want to go for a new record but to simply whip up a whopper of a lefse that would be a wee bit smaller than the world record. The goal would be to honor the Boys of Starbuck and to gain hands-on appreciation for the complexity and enormity of making a lefse big enough to cover a small car.

Larry paused. "Well, I'm the only one left," he said. "The rest of the guys have passed on."

Larry's news wasn't entirely surprising. Back in 1992 the Boys were a merry group of old guys who got a little goofy at times. At this point in my life, I could relate. The news saddened me. It was the first of many times in writing this second lefse book when equal amounts of grief and gratitude flooded my heart as I reflected on the past 25 years.

Just when I thought my idea seemed impossible, Larry started asking questions. He had some interest, but he also had reservations about who would be on the new team, who would cover costs, and how townspeople would take to the idea. Finally, we agreed to talk more when I came to visit his bakery in Starbuck.

Back to Starbuck

It was my first trip to Starbuck since the release of *The Last Word on Lefse.* As I drove on Highway 28 through Glenwood and into Starbuck, the view from high above Lake Minnewaska was magnificent. Starbuck still had its charm, even on this dark and stormy August day. When I met Larry, who was now 79 years old, at his bakery, he was making rosettes and wearing shorts, a gold chain around his neck, and a white baseball cap with LEFSE DAGEN in red letters. In his office was an unframed certificate honoring the Pastry Shoppe with membership into the Lefse Hall of Fame.

Larry offered coffee and rosettes, and we talked a little lefse. He asked if I planned a trip to Mrs. Olson's Lefse. I said I had an appointment with owner Mark Edevold. "It's really something to see how they make lefse there," said Larry. "Mark's got everything automated. It's unbelievable! The lefse is made in an old schoolhouse about five miles north of Gonvick, Minnesota. It's good lefse; it's just that it's not round."

We circled around to my idea of re-creating the World's Largest Lefse. Long story short, the answer was *no*. He was interested, and the Starbuck powers that be saw possibilities for good publicity for Lefse Dagen. But the general feeling was Starbuck already had the record in the Norwegian *Schibsted Book of Records* (according to the sign posted at the Starbuck Depot), so why risk embarrassment by taking on such a huge project again?

That was that. It was disappointing, and yet I had done what I could. I felt confident that all parts of the project were doable—except one, the grill. Eli Slabaugh said he could make the grill at his nearby shop, Glenwood Welding & Fabrication Inc. Cost: $1,500 to $2,000. I gulped. So when the project was shut down before it even started, it was a relief.

For Old Time's Sake

I soothed my disappointment with another rosette and more coffee. And then, much like a kid who's heard a favorite family story countless times but wants to hear it again, I asked Larry about the making of the World's Largest Lefse. I wasn't interested in the whole story, just parts of it that still puzzled or intrigued me after all these years. He grinned and moved his cap back on his head.

Legwold: *The dough for this monster lefse was made up of 30 pounds of potatoes, right?*
Larry: Right, instant potatoes. Potato Buds. We also used flour (35 pounds), sugar (1 pound), powdered milk (1 pound), and shortening (4 pounds).

Legwold: *On the wall of the Starbuck Depot museum is a very long and thin lefse stick. It looks like a crew oar, like someone had tapered the ends of a 2-by-12 to make a lefse stick for the record lefse.*
Larry: I looked at that and said, "You're not going to pick up a big lefse with a stick like that." We needed a big, thick rolling pin to carry the round. Maurice Walline made it with ⅜-inch-thick pine slats nailed around seven plywood circles, each with a 1-foot diameter. It hangs on the museum wall right below that lefse stick. We never would have been able to do the big lefse without that roller.

Legwold: *In the week before the actual event, you had two practice times. Why?*
Larry: We didn't want to look like idiots. We put plywood on a hay-rack and covered the plywood with a sheet. The first practice night, we rolled with regular 3-foot-long pins from the bakery. And when we had the lefse all rolled out, we put it on the big roller. When we hauled it over to the grill, it fell apart. We tried it on a second practice night and added puff-paste shortening used to make apple turnovers. It helped hold the dough together. We chilled the dough well, and used more charcoal to get more heat under the grill. So the second practice went better.
We didn't do another trial with the puff-paste shortening in

Larry Kittelson, front left, enjoys fame as one of the rollers of the World's Largest Lefse in 1983.

"World's Largest Lefse"

the dough. It was like, "This here will work or else." I figured it would work on the day of the event, and it worked like a charm.

Legwold: How thin was the world-record lefse?
Larry: About as thin as that napkin there. It wasn't thick by any means, like the thickness of two normal lefse stacked on top of each other.

Legwold: Did it bubble up on the grill?
Larry: Yep, just like regular lefse.

Legwold: After you accomplished the feat of making the record lefse, why not quit? Why did you try again right away—especially when that second one fell apart?
Larry: I made a batch twice the amount we needed, and I wanted to use up the damn dough. I didn't want to waste the rest of the batch. That second time didn't work as good, but luck was on our side with the first one.

Legwold: Other towns like Clarkfield and Madison [both in Minnesota] called for information on how to beat your record, right? What did you say to them?
Larry: An outfit from Washington state also called, and they wanted to try to break our record. I think I even gave them my recipe. I don't remember. I probably didn't give them the secret about the puff paste (laughs).

Legwold: Did this event put Starbuck on the map?
Larry: It sure did for a while. It really helped. You know, anything a small town can do nowadays to get itself on the map helps. We had the World's Largest Lefse and Heritage Days in 1983, and Lefse Dagen started in 1987. That record lefse brings a lot of people to town. It gives us some bragging rights.

Lefse pride is on parade in Starbuck, Minnesota!

I think it probably took me, oh, 20 to 25 years to finally feel like I sort of got the hang of making lefse. During that time I watched my mother-in-law, Hazel Nelson. I took her recipe, which was on a 3-by-5-inch card, and turned it into a long narrative I now share with my kids.

—Bill Wilson, 69, Scotts Mills, Oregon

10 LITTLE-KNOWN FACTS ABOUT THE WORLD'S LARGEST LEFSE

1. Julius Aaberg provided the two 5-by-10-foot, ¼-inch-thick steel plates that made up the grill. Arne Gorder (son of John Gorder, one of the Boys of Starbuck) welded the plates.
2. A crane transported the heavy, welded grill from Aaberg's ironworks across town to the site where the record lefse was rolled.
3. After onlookers crowded the Boys too much during the first practice night, spectators were cordoned off to allow the Boys room to work.
4. Three railroad rails, one on each side of the grill and one down the middle, held the grill above the charcoal bed that provided heat. The Boys ignited the coals three hours before showtime and placed the grill above the coals one hour before they began frying lefse. The Boys knew the grill was hot enough when they sprayed water and it bubbled and steamed. Maurice Amundson quipped, "Spraying was better than spitting."

5. To slide the grill into position, three Boys pulled a chain attached to the grill and two others used steel poles to push. They used trowels to lift the edge of the record lefse to see if the underside was done.

6. The 70-pound record lefse was draped over the huge transport pin and carried to the grill by four of the Boys.

7. Larry Kittelson had to jump up on the hayrack rolling surface to roll from his knees and get the round to its final record size. Larry's position was good for praying that the lefse would hold together on its journey to the grill.

8. The 8-by-16-foot hayrack that served as the rolling surface was later covered with a lace tablecloth. Audrey Amundson and Joyce Wallquist used this table to butter, sugar, and serve sections of the record lefse to the hundreds of spectators. The women wore fancy hats of the 1880s. Candleholders and vases of roses on the table added a touch of class to the occasion. All the lefse was eaten on the spot.

9. The Norwegian *Schibsted Book of Records* held up publication in 1983 until after the making of the World's Largest Lefse.

10. Judy Pederson, standing on a ladder above the crowd, filmed the record event using an 8mm camera.

"I'm glad I took the tape," she said. "I wanted to make sure that other people got to see it. This is something for our heritage."

Larry Kittelson is the last of the Boys of Starbuck who rolled the 1983 lefse.

10
Barnesville, Minnesota

When I roll my dough balls that have not been chilled, I think of the Norwegian ladies in heaven looking down and saying, "You can't do it that way! Those are warm potatoes!" But I figure my mother-in-law, Ethel Olson, is also looking down and maybe smiling.

—Jean Olson, 72, Deerwood, Minnesota

Pity the poor potato. It's packed with flavor and nutrition, and yet typically people display pathetically little potato appreciation. They deem it to be lowly and grubby, and they disparage the dirty little tuber, using phrases like "small potatoes" and "couch potato." The spud doesn't see the light of day until it's

A potato-picking contest started Potato Days in 1938.

Antique potato planting and harvesting equipment displays are part of Potato Days.

yanked from the muck, sliced, fried, mashed, riced, rolled, or whipped—and then greedily gobbled up.

Thankfully, there are people in our midst who find the potato to be most appealing. A.A. Milne, who wrote books about the thoughtful and steadfast Winnie-the-Pooh, praised the potato right proper when he wrote, "What I say is that, if a man really likes potatoes, he must be a pretty decent sort of fellow."

Pardon the promotional potato preamble (I lose perspective regarding potatoes), but it helps explain why we are in Barnesville. Lefse lovers are pretty decent folks who applaud the *pomme de terre,* holding it high because it is the fundamental ingredient in the most fantastic food this side of heaven. When it's lefse time, it's tater time—and it's tater time *all* the time during one potato-packed weekend in this northern Minnesota town (pop. 2,570 in 2013). Barnesville's annual Potato Days Festival in late August pulls in around 20,000 spud lovers who participate in events that embrace all things potato—including the National Lefse Cook-off. With good food, kooky contests, silly stuff you have to see to believe, and a gripping lefse competition, Barnesville's food festival is a must stop on the Lefse Trail.

Mashed-Potato Wrestling?

The Potato Days Festival website is peppered with plays on words (spud-tacular, spec-taters, a-peeling) that describe nearly 60 events that take place on Friday and Saturday. "Virtually everything you could possibly do to a potato is done over the two days," says the website. "Pick it, peel it, toss it, fry it, race it, bake it; but most of all, enjoy it."

The potato picking and peeling contests started the festival in 1938 and are still going strong. There's also the Miss Tater Tot Pageant, mashed potato and raw potato sculpturing, a potato cook-off, the search for a hidden golden potato, and a contest to see how fast two-man teams can sew and stack ten 100-pound bags of potatoes (record is 2 minutes, 55 seconds). Then the Potato Strong Man Contest challenges burly guys to heave the 100-pound bags as high as possible. Potato car races are for kids 5 to 11 years old. Whist and pinochle tournaments attract older adults.

Mashed-potato wrestling is an oh-so-appealing splash in a shallow pond of soupy spuds!

For the sports-minded, the festival offers potato runs (5K, 10K) and mashed-potato wrestling. Since its debut in 1999, mashed-potato wrestling has been one of the more popular events. Ah, there must be something primal and oh-so-appealing about splashing in a shallow pond of soupy spuds! Spectators gather three-deep in the Assumption Catholic Church parking lot to cheer for competitors 12 and younger, and for wrestlers in the 13-and-older category. Two-person teams grapple in a ring fashioned out of hay bales and tarps and then filled with mashed potatoes. Each pair wrestles two 3-minute rounds with a 60-second break between rounds. A T-shirt is awarded to each participant.

For the style-minded, the potato-sack fashion show features tuxedos, bathing suits, wedding gowns, and bib overalls. Superheroes are the focus of the fashion show in 2017.

There's a quilt show, parade, street dancing, and various other entertainment. An antique car show is a big draw, as are the crafts, shopping for Potato Days memorabilia, and food. In addition to standard festival fare (burgers, tacos, barbecued pork sandwiches, French fries, corn on the cob, malts), you can fill up on rommegrot, mashed potatoes, potato dumplings, potato-chip cookies, potato donuts, potato pancakes, potato sausage ... and lefse.

National Lefse Cook-off

At 9:30 a.m. on the festival's opening Friday, cook-off chair Margaret Ann Thompson and 15 volunteers prepare for visitors to Hildebrand Hall, a one-story building next to Assumption Catholic Church. In a space near the kitchen, they set up tables for selling and serving coffee, lemonade, and commercial lefse. They arrange the room where three judges will sit behind a closed door, soberly emptying their minds and clearing their palates so they can see, smell, feel, and taste the best of the best lefse. Inside a kitchen large enough to serve a hall the size of a basketball court, volunteers prep the rolling-and-grilling areas, which fill four long counters along the walls and a center island. The kitchen has room for up to 12 contestants to make lefse.

Contestants start arriving around 10 a.m., schlepping their own grills, rolling boards, flour bins, rolling pins, lefse sticks—whatever they need to make lefse in the hour-long competition. All contestants pay a $10 fee and must register before the event. Some are solo artists, and some have an entourage of family, friends, and groupies wearing identical T-shirts or bib aprons (not a requirement). Some contestants are teens, and a few have been in their 90s. Many compete yearly, renewing friendships and enjoying the camaraderie of other lefse makers (but keeping mum about their secret ingredients and techniques). Most contestants are women. Since 1996 when the cook-offs began, four men have won. Three-time winner Morris Howland was rolling strong in his 90s (see "Morrie, No More," page 101).

Margaret Ann Thompson chairs the National Lefse Cook-off.

Brother and sister Ben and Emma Bjerke entered their first-ever lefse contest in 2016 and won!

It takes a special breed of Norskie to compete in a lefse contest. First of all, *lefse contest* seems like an oxymoron. Just seeing the two words next to each other jams my gears. Lefse has such sweet associations of loved ones blissfully sharing their time and the bounty of communal cooking. Other individuals enjoy rolling away the day in their own little kitchen sanctuary, lost in memories and meditations. How does the leader-of-the-pack, dog-eat-dog drive of competition appeal to a shy, reticent Norskie?

Hmmm … maybe these lefse contestants are *really* a special breed of Norskies, hybrids of some sort, specially bred for big-time competition!

"Well, I don't know!" exclaimed Margaret Ann, playing along with this notion. "You might question how they could be in public like this if they are Norwegians, who are quiet and laid back. Maybe there's a part of them that *isn't* all Norwegian!"

"Is a background check in order?" I said. "Or maybe these Norwegians are as fiercely competitive as their Viking ancestors. They may be quiet, but they are determined to conquer and rule Lefse Land. Think about *that!*"

Judges Maureen Berg, Pat Rudie, and Sarah Montplaisir are all smiles during the judging process.

"Ha, ha, ha, ha, ha, ha, ha ... ah, yes," she said. Margaret Ann has a hearty, infectious laugh. "I think the most exciting part is watching the generations working together on this. That is really neat, like when a woman rolls with her great-grandkids or a granddaughter competes with her grandmother."

Throughout the morning, clutches of festivalgoers drift into a room in the hall to check out the quilt show. When the cook-off begins at 1 p.m., the lure of lefse becomes irresistible, and a crowd of up to 60 spectators gathers in front of the open window to the kitchen. They buy lefse to eat and settle in to study the contestants.

The contestants have one hour to make as many lefse as they can (usually around 20). They hope the lefse gods will smile on them and guide their hands to roll and grill one perfect lefse—the contest judges require only one. Officials call out the time remaining after 30 minutes and again after 50 minutes. Though the contestants are intent on winning, they enliven the kitchen with laughter, good-natured banter, and even singing on occasion.

On schedule, at 2 p.m., lefse sticks are dropped and grills unplugged. The contestants submit their best piece of lefse to the judges. While awaiting the results, some roll out what remains of their batch. Some let spectators try their hand at rolling and grilling. Before long, everyone is cleaning up and packing up. An emcee interviews contestants, who introduce their family and tell their lefse stories.

Meanwhile, the sequestered judges have an hour to evaluate every submission in order to make the tough calls. When they agree on the winners, judges usually skedaddle before the emcee announces results. Most contestants take the news in stride no matter what the outcome, chuckled Margaret Ann, but judges want to be long gone in case someone who finishes out of the money starts squawking. Prizes are $200 for cook-off champ, $100 for runner-up, and $50 for third place.

Millie and Cal Moen

One contestant who has been known to squawk at results is Millie Moen. Millie, 92, and her husband, Cal, 90, team up yearly in the National Lefse Cook-off. Last year this dynamic and delightful duo took third place. Still, you might say Millie is of a mind that, when it comes to lefse cook-offs, Justice is not only blind, but it also apparently lacks the ability to taste.

On a mild, gray November day, I met Margaret Ann at the Barnesville home of Millie and Cal. They were rolling lefse. A decade before, Margaret Ann had recruited Millie and Cal to be cook-off contestants. As we all talked while Millie and Cal rolled and grilled, it was easy to pick up on their sense of humor. I took a chance and asked about their issues with the cook-off judging.

"Is there something kinda goofy about the judging?" Millie asked Margaret Ann. "I shouldn't ask you, but it seems like kids can have any size or shape or anything, and they win the prizes."

"Next time, Millie, we have to pray about which lefse to turn in," said Cal, who is the griller. "Something like, 'Lord, show me the right lefse.'"

"In Barnesville here," said Millie, the roller, "everybody tells us we make the best lefse …"

"They wouldn't tell you otherwise, would they?" said Cal.

"… and then we got third last year and second 10 years ago," said Millie.

"The ones who win put quite a bit of sugar in their lefse," theorized Cal.

Cal and Millie Moen are still competing strong in their 90s.

"I want to win first place at least once before I retire," said Millie. "I won first at the Clay County Fair but never at Barnesville."

I wanted to remove Margaret Ann from the hot seat, so I asked Millie if she had a lefse-making tip or two. It took a moment to shift from pleading her case to passing on lefse advice. "Never give up trying," she said while continuing to roll. "I also do this with my pizza cutter." Millie demonstrated her tip.

TIP: If a round has ragged edges, trim them with a pizza cutter and save the scraps. When another round is ragged, fill the gaps by pressing the extra pieces to the round with a small roller. After grilling, the patchwork is difficult to detect.

Cal mentioned he played nine holes of golf that morning, walking the Willow Creek Golf Course. Amazing! I asked if he had other 90-year-old friends who played golf and walked the course. "Most of them have quit," said Cal. "I enjoy it even if I don't do well. One year I only played twice, riding the cart. I fell on the ice going out to get the mail and broke my hip. I've had five surgeries. They say you can't keep a good man down."

Cal and Millie were married in 1986, two years after her first husband, Jerome Silarud, died. She first learned to make lefse from Jerome's family. "At Christmastime in 1946 or 1947," recalled Millie, "Jerome and I were going to make lefse on the kitchen range that had the holes on top. We were making lefse for the first time in our first home, and things were not going well. The dough was too moist, too sticky. He kept telling me what to do, until I got so upset I took a lefse dough ball and threw it at him."

"Did you hit him?" I asked, laughing at the image of a man ducking a high-and-tight dough ball.

"I suppose I did. He was a mild-mannered man, like the one I have now. I didn't learn how to make lefse very much then. It's really been since I married Cal that I've made all this lefse."

When the dynamic duo was done with the lefse making, they offered me a round to butter and sprinkle with sugar. Delish! Millie then gave Margaret Ann and me each a sealed bag containing several rounds. Margaret Ann said her gift was going to go directly to her farmhands, who were combining corn that day.

Before leaving I was hoping for a final dose of Millie's humor when I asked, "When did you hit your stride and become really good at this lefse making?"

"Yesterday."

Lefse Queen Jean

I met Jean Olson, 72, at her home in Deerwood, Minnesota, where she is known as the Queen of Lefse. Queen Jean was barefoot and rolling lefse while wearing a white T-shirt with the words "Show Me The Lefse!" on the front. Every year she makes 1,000 circles for Crosby's Immanuel Lutheran Church fall fundraiser. She also takes private orders, charging $1.50 a round.

Jean's Minnesota car license plate says LEFSEQN. "When my husband, Adrian Olson, drives my car to Dubuque," said Jean, laughing, "I wonder what people in Iowa think when they see that license plate and then see him driving."

Jean won the National Lefse Cook-off in 2005, the first year she entered. "I'd never been in a contest before," she recalled, "and I probably was a little nervous. People like my lefse, but I wondered what would it be like to compete. ... *Nobody* talked to anybody that year. It was like, 'I'm not going to tell you any of my secrets because if I win I don't want you to know them.'

"It was fun to be able to see all the spectators, who are talking the whole time. My first round failed, and there were whispers. After rolling that first one, though, it was a matter of, 'Just relax. Take your time.' I rolled 25 in that hour. And with 10 grills going, it was a lot of uneven power. I chose my best, which was kinda hard, and I was shocked when they announced I was the winner."

Jean would never have predicted a lefse championship in her future when she first made lefse. What a madcap misfortune! When she saw a newspaper recipe calling for instant potatoes, she and her husband tried it. "It turned out like wallpaper paste," she said. "I added more potatoes, and that was no help. Then I added more flour, and that was no help. This went on a while, and finally we threw it out. The two of us struggled to carry the garbage can out; it was that heavy."

For the annual church fundraiser and her private orders, Jean makes lefse from 300 pounds of potatoes donated yearly by a friend, who gets all the lefse he wants in exchange. She moves easily in her kitchen and is a natural teacher as she rolls and grills. She's also a wellspring of lefse-making tips. Here are five:

Jean Olson, the Lefse Queen, won the National Lefse Cook-off the first year she entered.

TIP: "For a beginner, don't do more than 5 pounds of potatoes. That's a lot of lefse to roll. Go for the smaller circles but try to keep them round, rather than trying to make big ones like grandma used to make and then ending up with lefse shaped like the state of Texas."

TIP: Cool lefse on a towel placed over a cookie-cooling rack. Lifting the towel, Jean said, "See the moisture that forms underneath? The rack helps the lefse get rid of excess moisture that can make freezing a mess."

TIP: "Before freezing, wrap six cooled-and-folded rounds in Saran Wrap. Wait 24 hours, and then put the lefse in a Ziploc bag for freezing."

TIP: If you don't have time to peel and cook the potatoes at once, "you can peel the potatoes and cover with water, adding 1 tablespoon of lemon juice. When you're ready to boil the potatoes, drain the pot, add fresh water, and cook."

Jean's last tip is a bit of a jaw-dropper. You see, cooling lefse dough overnight in a refrigerator is standard practice among makers of potato lefse. Well, Queen Jean is really a rebel in disguise because she advocates *not* cooling the dough overnight! "I used to do that but didn't like the way the potatoes rolled when cold," she said. "Several years ago before my mother-in-law, Ethel Olson, passed away, we both changed our minds on how cold the potatoes needed to be." So this is her **TIP:** "Letting the warm dough cool at room temperature for not more than two or three hours is sufficient. Let the dough cool until it's still somewhat warm to touch—not hot, though. This makes balls that roll nicer."

This tip is a tough sell in Lefse Land, but I have tried it and now prefer to roll slightly warm dough. Consider me a convert. The caveat is the dough can be too warm and get sticky. But the more you work with this concept and enjoy the easier rolling and the reduced prep time, the more you'll know how to handle the dough.

Handling the doubters, on the other hand, is not as easy. "Oh, I face the scorn and wrath of the Norwegian lefse ladies," said Jean, "but the proof is in the pudding."

We hosted a lefse lesson in our kitchen for the Normandale Community College chemistry department, where my husband, Earl, worked. I was a very difficult taskmaster; I wouldn't let them goof off, except we did do some dancing when we were rolling. I wouldn't let them taste a beverage until we were done. They wanted to drink beer in my kitchen while we were baking lefse in my class! This was a lesson, you see; I am a teacher also, and I was pretty tough that day. They are still talking about how mean I was. But the students gave me a lefse stick that I still use. It says "Master Lefse Maker." I don't think one of them makes lefse today. Not one. Did I scare them away? I don't know. I tried not to. No, we had a good time.

—Shirley Evenstad, 71, Minneapolis

MORRIE, NO MORE

When I interviewed three-time cook-off champion Morris Howland, it was the last time he made lefse. He passed away a few months after the interview, four months short of his 97th birthday.

After Jean Olson, the Lefse Queen, talked up this legendary lefse champ, I immediately called him and left messages over the next few weeks. I had heard he had bounced back from lung cancer but then had struggled through bouts of pneumonia.

When Morrie and I finally connected by phone, he sounded weak but game for an interview at least. Maybe he could muster enough energy to also roll and grill lefse. "I run down the hall as fast as I can walk," he quipped.

The interview occurred in early December at his apartment in Ortonville, Minnesota. To my surprise, he opened the door wearing a red apron that said "Lefse Maker Morrie" and a poofy red chef's hat that also said "Lefse Maker."

Morrie was rolling lefse with a 150-year-old pin inherited from his mother, Mathilda Howland. Though winded, he still had it as a roller. With a light touch, he rolled the dough methodically, rotating the pastry board every few passes in order to get round rounds. Rubber bands held a pastry sock to the rolling pin. Between rounds, Morrie rolled the pin back and forth across the board so the sock picked up flour.

After just 20 minutes, Morrie stopped making lefse. "I used to have the energy to do these things, that little extra *oomph* to do 75 rounds and not get pooped," he said. "Now I did eight. You learn to accept slowing down. It comes naturally."

We sat a spell. He said the first time he entered the National Lefse Cook-off, he blew it by adding flour to his dough before traveling to Barnesville, Minnesota, for the competition. "You don't do that," he said with a wry smile. He tried rolling a few rounds and then

When in his 90s, Morrie Howland won the National Lefse Cook-off three straight years.

withdrew. The next year he tied for second place, and then he became the Baron of Barnesville, winning the next three years straight. "When I did it three times in a row, I thought, 'Why break the buggy?'" he said. "If I came out ahead three times, why test it for a fourth? So after that I went as a critic"— and a celebrity. He was often introduced to spectators and interviewed by the cook-off emcee.

Over the years, Morrie made care packages of lefse, krumkake, flatbread, and Swedish toast for rest-home residents. He helped his church, First English Lutheran, make lefse for its yearly bazaar. But he quit after his wife, Alice, died and organizers, struggling to find workers, switched to Potato Buds. "Not the real McCoy," he said. "I will not do anything that isn't *legal*. Well, of course, Potato Buds are legal, but then your potatoes are not from raw ingredients; they are processed beforehand. I do not think they're as good, and I will not work with them."

As a boy, Morrie helped his mother make lefse for holiday lutefisk dinners. "Oh yes, the butter would roll down to your elbows as you put the lutefisk on your lefse," Morrie recalled fondly. Nowadays, he told me, his treat was thin lefse wrapped around cold shrimp with cocktail sauce. "That and a glass of white wine—lovely!" he said, beaming.

I asked how he had lived so long. He laughed. "Genes. My mother lived to be 102. That and I'd have a big glass of tomato juice—pure—every morning. I had a big garden and put up 100 quarts of tomato juice a year. Yep, tomato juice gives you a lot of get up and go."

What gave Morrie gladness was giving to others. "Last year I was able to put together those four-item care packages at Christmas," he said. "People in the rest home sometimes are not very mobile. How else do they get treats like that, treats they were accustomed to in their younger days? It was a pleasure to be able to give them treats. You know, that makes a person's heart feel pretty good. It isn't just the giving; it's what it gives you. It gives me joy."

It gave me joy to spend time with Morrie. He also gave me some lefse, Swedish toast, and his lefse recipe:

- **6   cups russet potatoes, mashed and riced**
- **1   cup whipping cream**
- **½   cup butter**
- **2   tablespoons sugar**
- **1   teaspoon salt**

"There you got it," he said. "I mix it up and put it in the fridge overnight. I use 3 cups of flour, and I do half the flour with half the mix. And then I do the other half of the flour with the other half of the mix. And I don't do the batch any quicker than I have to."

His parting advice to lefse makers—and perhaps his message for life: Practice patience. "I learned quickly that if you didn't want to throw the whole batch away, you have to slow down."

Asked how he lived so long, Morrie said, "Genes. My mother lived to be 102. That and I'd have a big glass of tomato juice—pure—every morning."

11
Gonvick, Minnesota

*There are different ways to make lefse,
and there's no one way better than the next.
We're all in support of making lefse
no matter how we make it. If the end result
is that people enjoy it, including the maker,
then that's what it's all about.*

—David Hofstad, 75, Cheverly, Maryland

Consider the square. Beyond Lefse Land's borders, square is celebrated, as in "fair and square," "square meal," and "square deal." But in Lefse Land, square is spurned, rebuffed in a world ruled by the holy round. Rolling pins are round. Pastry boards are round. And with lefse, of course, round is held in high regard.

Now consider Gonvick (pop. 284 in 2013), where we stop on the Lefse Trail to do an eye-popping tour of the Winsor Products Co. Lefse Factory. Winsor has made Mrs. Olson's Lefse since 1959. The company has not just survived but also thrived as the only manufacturer of lefse known far and wide as *square*. They dance to the beat of a different drum up here in this northern Minnesota outpost, and there's not a round to be found among Mrs. Olson's Lefse. Heck, the company theme song could very well be "Hip To Be Square" by Huey Lewis and the News.

> *Don't tell me that I'm crazy*
> *Don't tell me I'm nowhere*
> *Take it from me*
> *It's hip to be square*
> *It's hip to be square*
> *It's hip to be square*
> *It's hip to be square.*

I seemed to have arrived in the middle of nowhere after driving four and a half hours north from Minneapolis to this wide-open, windswept part of the state. Mrs. Olson's factory is five miles north of Gonvick. An antique dough mixer with a large bowl under an inverted L-shaped mixing motor marked its driveway. The two-story building was originally Winsor School, built in 1917 for elementary school children. Owners Mark Edevold, 56, and his dad, Ron Edevold, 77, greeted me. Both were wearing white hairnets.

"It's so far up here," I said, walking off the stiffness from the road trip.

"Yeah," said Ron, "but it's so much fun when you get here."

Ron was right. Touring Mrs. Olson's turned out to be a kick—and a lesson in the perils of prejudging. It was a kick because it was exactly as Starbuck's Larry Kittelson had said when he called this resource-fully automated lefse factory "unbelievable!" The tour taught me, for the umpteenth time, to judge not. My expectations had been low because of my highfalutin prejudice against square lefse. Also, I had a bias against machine-made lefse. Only people should make lefse, I believed, just as only Paul Bunyan should cut down trees—not some

Ron Edevold, left, and son Mark Edevold show Mrs. Olson's products. Behind them, large dough balls are ready to be fed into Mrs. Olson's unique lefse-making machine.

newfangled "steam saw" (the folktale's term for chainsaw). But in the middle of the tour, I admitted to the Edevolds: "You guys know what you're doing! Here I thought I was going to find a gimmicky, mom-and-pop lefse joint, but you've put a lot of thought into engineering your way toward labor-saving efficiency."

Endless Lefse

Mrs. Olson's process starts with a hay-bale elevator that carries 40-pound bags of Idaho potato flakes to the attic of the factory. Three times daily, a worker "feeds the beast," said Ron, by dumping potato flakes into a large bin that supplies a hopper on the main floor. The hopper serves a mixer where the potato flakes first combine with powdered milk, salt, sorbic acid (a mold inhibitor derived from berries of the mountain ash tree), and then flour and water to form a batch of dough weighing 160 pounds.

George Herberg, Ron's stepfather, invented the lefse-making machine 56 years earlier. "We've built and rebuilt this thing so many times," said Ron. "It really works well now. Each 160-pound batch takes about 15 minutes to cook and cool. We make a new batch about every 15 minutes, and we do 30 or more batches a day. Not all year-round, but we do after Labor Day with the start of our season. We have 12 employees working during the season, which stops right around Christmastime. We have orders throughout the year, but nothing like now through Christmas."

Here is how the machine works: A worker divides each batch into 10 watermelon-shaped spheres and feeds each one into a small hopper at the starting point of the lefse-making machine. Workers must continuously feed warm dough "melons" into the hopper. From this steady supply of dough, hopper rollers squeeze out a thin, straight-sided line of lefse about 1 foot wide. The lefse rides a metal track inches above a 40-foot trail of blue gas flames. Moving steadily, the track twists and turns and manages to cook both sides of the lefse. Then the cooked lefse cools over a space

Workers package the squared lefse.

without flames before entering a 10-foot-tall refrigerator, where the heat that remains in the lefse is removed. Cooled lefse emerges from the tower and goes through a machine that cuts the lefse into squares. The transformation from dough to finished lefse takes about four minutes.

Pointing to the hopper at the starting point, Ron said, "It's a cardinal sin to let that hopper run out. If it goes empty, then we have to shut it down and start all over again. That's a terrible feeling, and it happened to me once. I was doing something else, and I looked over there, and there was no lefse in the line."

I asked why the dough did not stick to the rollers. "That's a secret," Ron said. "Working that out didn't happen overnight, either."

I speculated that the secret must be in the dough's formulation. Ron smiled. "That's part of it."

We moved quietly along the line. Mark was busy brushing off pieces of lefse that could stick to the track. It struck me that workers didn't have to make decisions about how big to roll the lefse, when to turn the lefse on the grill, and when to pull the lefse when it was done. This machine did all that. Workers came into play only to make dough, feed it into the machine, and package and ship the finished lefse squares.

Ron nodded toward the cutter that chops the lefse line into sheets. "I built the cutter," he said. "We used to have triangle-shaped lefse, and I built an X cutter that made the triangles." He shook his head and mumbled that triangles were a bother.

There are 10 lefse squares per package, and each package is sealed by hand and fed onto a revolving turntable. Plastic dividers on the turntable force the packages under a machine that automatically sprays a sell-by date onto the package. Dated packages are boxed and shipped from a warehouse the Edevolds built onto the schoolhouse in 1992. Mrs. Olson's ships orders of six or twelve 16-ounce packages to individuals, retailers, and wholesalers nationwide but primarily to lefse lovers in Minnesota, the Dakotas, Wisconsin, and Iowa.

Name Change Changes Fortunes

We moved inside the office to talk without production noises and without wearing hairnets. Ron said the product started as Winsor Lefse because Gonvick is in Winsor Township. Winsor

Mark Edevold and Carolyn Rude work a turntable that automatically sprays a sell-by date onto the package.

isn't much of a Scandinavian name, so owners Laura and George Herberg, Ron's mother and stepfather, changed the name to Mrs. Olson's Lefse. "If you remember, Mrs. Olson was advertising Folgers coffee," said Ron. "My folks were naïve. They thought they would get in trouble with Folgers for using Mrs. Olson's, but that's a generic name, Olson. There was no problem."

The new name opened doors with food brokers, and sales jumped. "It got us into all the warehouses in Minnesota, Montana, North Dakota, Washington state, and Wisconsin," said Ron. "That was a big turning point."

In 1984 Ron, at age 44, took over Mrs. Olson's. He had been a safety engineer in Colorado after studying physics and math at the University of Minnesota and Bemidji State University. "Production was 100 percent different than it is now," he said. "There were two machines, but they could only run one. It was the same type of machine that we have now, but it was really crude. The product they made wasn't that good, but it was good at the time. We developed a different shortening and a little bit different recipe, plus we brought uniformity to the product."

Thinking Outside the Round

This idea of using invention to make uniform lefse for the sake of efficiency is what has driven Mrs. Olson's to go beyond the round borders of Lefse Land—and draw fire because of it. "It's more productive to make a single strip than it is to make lots of individual lefse rounds," said Mark. "As far as for the consumer, it's better because we can offer a better price. We're a lot less labor intensive."

Mark added that Mrs. Olson's has a broad distribution, so it's easy to find in stores. "We private label it with a lot of companies, so we sell a lot of it. The advantage is we have a consistent product. It's always the same texture, moisture, and flavor. Again, the price is pretty good. We probably sell a little bit too cheap, but we sell. None of this putting the product out there and it sits, you know?"

While Mark stepped out to go to the freezer, Ron told me they sell to cruise ships where Norwegian chefs make hors d'oeuvres using lefse and a salmon spread. He added that the Four Seasons Hotels and Resorts orders lefse for making cream-cheese-

and-salmon pinwheel hors d'oeuvres. He also said something surprising: Some customers don't like round. "People who see our lefse like it because it is squared," he said. "It's easier to work with. It's easier to butter and roll up at the table."

Mark returned, holding two clear plastic bags, both examples of Mrs. Olson's ongoing innovation. One was Laura's Pumpkin Lefse, which is sold around Halloween. It is Mrs. Olson's Lefse with added pumpkin and spice. At Gonvick's Pumpkin Days, Mark said they sold pumpkin lefse topped with cream cheese and marshmallow cream, "and, oh boy, did customers like that!"

The other bag contained a dozen dough balls. "Gary, this is our newest incarnation," Mark said. "One of our problems is our lefse is good, but it's not homemade lefse. It doesn't have flour coating it, and it's not cooked and flipped and cooked and flipped. I'd like to add a floured surface component to our machine, like homemade, but it's really hard to do. If we had flour everywhere that was piling up on the floors and on the equipment, that would create a whole new set of problems.

"So anyway, one day I thought, 'Why don't we just portion out our dough, freeze it, and sell it in stores?' It's frozen, ready to roll, and you don't have to do any of the work of boiling the potatoes, ricing the potatoes, and all the rest. Just thaw these dough balls, spread flour on your countertop, roll it, fry it in a skillet or on a lefse griddle, and it really works well."

Mark had visions of supplying dough balls to street vendors. "They could roll them out into an 8-inch round and make a round into a cone. Then they'd put mashed potatoes in there, and put a hot dog in there with onions and

Mrs. Olson's ships nationwide but primarily to lefse lovers in Minnesota, the Dakotas, Wisconsin, and Iowa.

sauerkraut and grated cheese and ketchup, and away you go. Eat it with a fork and a spoon."

I'll take two of those!

My older brother, Donn Erickson, lived in Grand Forks, North Dakota. Donn's lefse recipe was outrageously different from anything we've ever tried or heard about in making lefse. He used Hungry Jack potato flakes, a bottle of 7-Up, a cup of evaporated milk, cold water, oil, and a little sugar, salt, and flour. My goodness, what a mixture that was! We did taste it. It was fine but certainly a very strange recipe.

–Elaine Wilson, 69, Scotts Mills, Oregon

LEFSE LINKED TO WITNESS-PROTECTION PROGRAM

"Do I feel a bond with other lefse makers?" said Dan Olson, 66, retired Minnesota Public Radio news reporter. "Sure! I don't know that much about you, but because you make lefse, you're a good guy."

That insight came early in my interview of Dan on a gray, brisk December day at the Spoonriver Restaurant in Minneapolis. A splash of wine there and later at his condo helped warm the day—and loosen the tongue.

"Lefse was a food, not some holiday thing twice a year," said

Dan. "Lefse was on the table a third of the year on the farm where I grew up in Halstad, Minnesota. Lefse was part of the menu. When my mother passed away and we cleaned out her freezer, there were packages of Olive Olson's lefse, labeled but forgotten, at the bottom of the freezer. Heartbreaking, because she made good lefse, especially when you added enough butter and sugar—which, of course, is pretty much what lefse is. Lefse is a conveyance for butter and sugar."

Dan Olson: "I don't know that much about you, but because you make lefse, you're a good guy."

Dan makes good lefse but scoffs at lefse makers who are puffed up by perfectionism. "Round lefse rounds are aesthetic things that snobby cooks really, really like and emphasize," he said. "But it's all about the taste. Actually, it's all about the process."

And the process sometimes includes mistakes. "I remember once when we used red potatoes," Dan said. "Can't use red potatoes. The dough turned into … what was the movie, *The Blob That Devoured New York*? Something like that. It was just a big, gooey, sticky, messy blob. You could have built a brick wall and used the dough as mortar.

"And then there was the time I forgot to put salt in one batch. That's when I uttered my first expletive in the presence of children—whose parents were quite religiously devout. I said something like, 'Oh, ----, I forgot the salt!' The children were fine with it; they were city kids. But the parents were stupefied."

Dan paused and stared at his wine glass, deep in thought. And then he just out and said it.

"Norway sends all of its most serious offenders into a witness-protection program—provided they agreed to turn state's evidence."

I stared at him, at this bolt out of the blue. He continued in the low voice that had become so familiar to MPR listeners.

"But of course with Norway being a small country, these offenders in the program are not especially safe there. The United States is a much larger country, and Minnesota is friendly to Norway. Therefore, Norway sends all of its witness-protection program people here to Minnesota."

Without a smile, he continued, tongue in cheek.

"Floyd B. Olson? Not his real name. Wendell Anderson? Not his real name. These are people—former Minnesota governors, mind you—placed here in Minnesota as part of the Norwegian witness-protection program. Every Olson you meet? All witness-protection program people."

Even him? Was this a confession, something Dan had to get off his chest?

"What offense did these people commit?" Dan asked. "Doesn't matter. A range of offenses we can't talk about, obviously. But you have to admit, it's a pretty safe name to hide under. Olson, Anderson, Johnson … yeah, we're all here."

Less than a month later, Dan was gone from the Minneapolis scene. Rumor has it the witness-protection program assigned Dan Olson, or whatever his name is, to Golden, Colorado. But I'm betting his cover will be blown once the lefse-making season begins.

12
West Fargo, North Dakota

I'm strictly butter only on my lefse. When my brother's wife joined the family, she wanted to put sugar on her round. We all looked at her and said, "Like what? What are you talking about?"
As a result, my son and others then wanted sugar. This year, my son tried honey on it and claimed it was the best thing he ever tasted! Whatever! Me? Butter only. I don't want the crunchy things or anything else on my lefse.

—Shirley Faa, 67, Minot, North Dakota

Freddy's Lefse Bakery in West Fargo is refreshing for three reasons:

1. Location. Freddy's is a stone's throw from Interstate 94, so it's easy-in, easy-out as you travel to and from such popular North Dakota destinations as Theodore Roosevelt National Park near the state's western border, the North Dakota Heritage Center and State Museum in Bismarck, and the Norsk Hostfest in Minot. Also, Freddy's does not offer tours, just good lefse and friendly conversation as you make your purchase and get back on the road in 10 minutes, tops. So look at this as the change-of-pace break on the Lefse Trail.

2. Packaging. The wording at the bottom of Freddy's plastic bag makes your mouth water. It states: "Serve with lutefisk, pork links, bacon, sausage or hamburger. Also delightful snack rolled up with butter, or butter and sugar, jelly or cinnamon. Excellent potato substitute for family lunch boxes."

3. Motto. "We've been frying to please you since 1946." Now, doesn't that little play on words make you smile and want to have some lefse?

I had my refreshing Freddy's break on the way to the Norsk Hostfest in late September. The lefse season was starting to rev up (to such a degree that Carl's Lefse in Hawley, Minnesota, had politely turned down my request for an interview). Therefore, I was thrilled to get an audience with Michelle Cox, 55, who oversees sales and production and everything else at Freddy's.

As I drove into West Fargo (pop. 31,771 in 2014), it dawned on me that Freddy's is the oldest lefse factory going. Fred and Lorraine Cox, bakers by trade, tried making potato chips, but in 1946 they switched to making lefse in the basement of their north Fargo home. Freddy's Lefse grew, which forced the business to move to a small neighborhood shop and employ local women. More growth led the Cox family to build a shop behind their home and finally to set up production at the current factory in West Fargo.

The sign says it all: Freddy's is a stone's throw from Interstate 94.

I pulled into the parking lot on the west side of a blue-and-gray warehouse, which Freddy's shares with McGarry's Barbershop and S.T.H. Auto Center. I entered Freddy's small customer waiting room, and soon Michelle appeared from a work area, which, she politely explained, was not open to the public.

Freddy's, which began in Fred and Lorraine Cox's basement, is the oldest lefse factory going.

It was almost closing time as Michelle and I took seats in her office, which had a dusting of flour on the floor. I joked that it was a surprise to find flour all about in a lefse factory. She smiled. She had been on her feet all day doing whatever needed to be done to make lots of good lefse. She was also breaking in a batch of new employees, so she seemed grateful for a chance to sit and talk lefse.

Legwold: *How did you get started in the lefse business?*
Michelle: I started working for my in-laws, Fred and Lorraine, who have passed on. I've been doing lefse my whole life since I was 18 years old.

Legwold: *Really, your entire professional life has been in making lefse? I don't think I've ever met a lefse lifer.*
Michelle: I think I've only tasted one other type of lefse my entire life. I was raised on this lefse, and the recipe has never changed. Before I ever got involved with Freddy's, my grandmother Alena O'Marro worked with them part-time for 15 years. So that was all I knew. It's been great. I love what I do. People always come in with a smile on their face. When they smell lefse cooking, they say, "Oh, it smells like my childhood!" It's always positive. So, yeah, I've been very pleased with the life of making lefse. I've never thought of doing anything else. This is what I know. This is what I'm good at.

Legwold: *Family-owned businesses are not always easy to manage, so it's amazing that the Cox family has run Freddy's for 70-some years.*
Michelle: This is my 37th year. And my husband, Terry Cox, has been doing it for 41 years. He works out of production. He's actually the main roller and one of the owners. He oversees my daughter, Amanda Lien, who has been working with us for 16 years. She's in production also. And Barry Cox, Terry's brother and the other owner, runs the kitchen. We all oversee everything, but in general Barry does the kitchen, Terry does a lot of the line work, Amanda helps with packaging and keeping things running—and I go wherever I have to be.

Legwold: *What do you like best about this business?*
Michelle: It's small, and I like the family aspect. Most people don't care to work with their family, but we've always done very well. I like that. And with the employees we get, they just kind of come into the fold. I get to be friends with them, and it's a nice atmosphere.

Legwold: *Michelle, I understand the need to keep your production methods to yourself, but I'm fascinated by how lefse is mass-produced. Could you give me a general idea of how Freddy's makes its lefse?*
Michelle: Years ago, we'd roll one lefse and take it over to fry on an individual grill. Now, Terry has made production efficient so people do particular jobs, like an assembly line. We have a conveyor belt with a machine roller that flattens the dough to about half its original thickness, to a thickness that's manageable for the people who roll and finish and shape the round. Usually there are two people who physically roll by hand.

Legwold: *So the machine roller on the line makes the human roller's job easier and faster.*
Michelle: My husband has developed our equipment, and over the years that has

Fred Cox in 1957.

helped us to make production more efficient. But the rolling is still 50 percent done by hand, and every piece is handled multiple times. It's not done by machine. People handle it. A machine roller couldn't get it the way we like it, or the way people expect it. Our finished lefse rounds are about the size of a dinner plate. They vary, of course. We tell people our lefse are like snowflakes; there are no two that are the same because they are done by hand. They are not going to be perfect all the time.

Legwold: Lefse making is hard work, right? You have long hours on your feet, working six (or more) days a week during the season, finding good employees, and meeting the demands of sometimes desperate lefse lovers nationwide.
Michelle: It's a lot of work. Anyone who doesn't think so is plumb crazy. Even with having some of our process being automated, it's still a lot of work, a lot of physical labor. The lefse is handled by hand a lot. People think that everything is done by machine nowadays. No. Some of our competitors are going down—I don't like to see that because there's room for everybody—because this is physical work and we lack employees who want to work and aren't afraid of work. Young people want to work with a machine. Very seldom do we get young people who will do the physical work. We don't ever get anybody under 30.

Legwold: With such shortage of willing workers, do you hire just about anybody?
Michelle: Yes. But you never know. You never judge a book by its cover. You just say, "OK, you want to give it a try? Let's give it a try." We have 12 to 15 employees during the season. We've got retired people who still know how to work and want to work—and we're happy to hire them if they want to do it.

Legwold: Is the lefse market growing?
Michelle: Other lefse companies have cut way back or died because of employment issues, so their customers are coming to Freddy's, in part. The demand is there, and our market is growing. We ship all over. If you could automate it all, you could supply a lot. It's endless what you could do. But we have found that we can't automate our

product enough to where we can cut way back on employees. It's still very much an employee-driven product. Employment is the biggest challenge because there are so many jobs available right now in town. We could double production if we knew we could hire people. But we can't.

Michelle Cox: "What's funny is we've had many women who serve Freddy's Lefse but don't tell their guests that it's ours."

Legwold: I don't think people outside of the lefse-making business can fully appreciate how lefse-crazed customers can get so wigged out when it's Thanksgiving or Christmas and they don't have their lefse yet.

Michelle: Oh, there is always that last-minute panic. We used to have the business in the house basement, and then we moved it to a shop next to the house. That's a very bad thing, to have your home right next to your business. We would be sitting down to Thanksgiving dinner, and the doorbell would ring. "We forgot to pick up our lefse!" We got to the point where we just had to stop answering the door. It was nice when we separated the business from our residence. Now we can walk away from it.

Legwold: Here's a tough question: How are lefse factories such as yours affecting the lefse market? I mean, because you produce good lefse, you make it easy for families not to roll and grill lefse at home. One could argue that you are contributing to the end of the lefse-making tradition.

Michelle: If lefse factories didn't make lefse, I don't think a lot of people would make it. Honestly, I don't think they would do it anymore. We have a lot of older people who come in and say, "Oh, thank God, now I don't have to do it." It's just easier when you can buy good lefse. What's funny is we've had many women who serve Freddy's Lefse but don't tell their guests that it's ours.

Legwold: *Are young people learning?*
Michelle: No. It is very sad because lefse making should be some-thing that's passed down, like making krumkake or pumpkin pie. You can't imagine how many people come in and say, "I have all the equipment, but I just can't find the time." Or "I have the equipment, but nobody taught me." But then there are others who get together as a family and have a great holiday tradition out of making lefse. That's fantastic!

Unless you teach your children and grandchildren that lefse is important and is the flavor of Thanksgiving and Christmas, lefse making will die out. I'm sure there are fewer people doing it now than there were 20 years back. Most young people won't even try to learn unless there is somebody encouraging them.

—Mary Lou Peterson, 71, Minnetonka, Minnesota

HERE'S TO HAZEL, 101

It was an honor to have talked lefse with 101-year-old Hazel Larsgaard, who passed away four months after I did this inter-view. It was sad to hear the news because elders like Hazel are such marvels, wellsprings of strength, faith, and inspiration.

Hazel and I had scheduled the interview for the Wednes-day after Election Day 2016. I thought about canceling but then nixed the idea. Driving to Hudson, South Dakota (pop. 316 in 2014), and sharing lefse stories would be the perfect antidote to what had been an ugly, divisive campaign sea-son. New bumper sticker: Unite USA? Ubetcha—Lefse!

The day was bright and breezy as I pulled into the care center in Hudson. Hazel's daughter Denise Koopsma joined us. Hazel had stopped making lefse about five years earlier when she had a heart-valve replacement, but the family tradition was in good hands with Denise.

It was lunchtime, and Denise just happened to bring lefse. The rounds had the prettiest edges I'd ever seen. The edges were uniformly wavy, cut with a pastry cutter and crimper. The tool made a half-round of lefse look like art, like a hand fan used by Norwegian royalty. It looked almost too pretty to eat. Almost.

When Denise offered lefse, I said sure. She buttered half-rounds and then pulled out another pleasant surprise: a silver spoon with a rim of small holes to allow sugar granules to sift through. Cool!

"I pride myself in making lefse just like Mom made hers," said Denise, "right down to grinding the potatoes with a hand-crank grinder. Mom also cut her lefse exactly round so every piece is the same. It's not necessary, but that's how I was raised to think all lefse should look." Hazel said she had learned from her mother, Rita Ragligaard, and Denise had learned from Hazel. That's how it works with traditions, right?

The lefse was excellent, though just to be in the presence of anyone 101 years old—especially a lefse maker—was pleasure enough. Since I don't get to talk with centenarians every day, I couldn't resist asking questions that, more

Denise Koopsma, right, likens herself to her mother, Hazel Larsgaard. "Mom always got things done. I get things done."

Hazel taught Denise to trim lefse edges with a pastry cutter and crimper.

than anything, seemed to amuse Hazel.

"How did you live so long?" I asked.

"Oh, I don't know," she giggled. "I never thought about it. One day at a time, I guess."

"Do you fear death?"

"No, I'm ready to go."

"What do you think happens after death?"

"It's a new life."

"What will that new life bring?"

"Well, I'll be up with Christ. That's about all I know about it. Gotta live your life right, then you're OK."

"Are you glad you have lived to 101?"

"I'm thankful for every day I have."

Denise was holding back tears. I asked if something was the matter. She shook her head but a moment later said, "I probably should have paid more attention, written more down when I was sure I'd get clear answers. The stories … the memory goes. I should have written them down."

I asked Denise if she was like Hazel. "Mom always got things done. I get things done," Denise said, tearing and laughing at the same time. "I don't know why it bothers me so much to even talk about that. I thought we were just going to talk about *lefse!*"

A few weeks later, I received an email from Denise explaining how heritage kicked in at this time of year and for her not making lefse at the holidays would be "unthinkable." Then she added this about Hazel: "Mom is sending a Christmas card this year with the picture of her birthday cake. … On the back of the card is a picture of Mom's hand on the Bible and the words printed below the picture: 'Let us hold tightly without wavering to the hope we affirm, for God can be trusted to keep his promise. Hebrews 10:23.'"

13
Minot, North Dakota

*If people are going to complain about
lefse not being perfectly round, I figure, hey,
they can see if they can do it.*

—Mary Lou Peterson, 71, Minnetonka, Minnesota

For many Scandinavians, the migration to Minot, North Dakota, for the Norsk Hostfest is an annual autumn pilgrimage. All things Scandinavian can be found there, including all kinds of commercial and homemade lefse—and even a friendly lefse competition. The Hostfest has earned its spot on the Lefse Trail.

Celebrating 40 years in September 2017, the Hostfest is America's largest Scandinavian festival. "We typically get ready for 55,000 to 60,000 people each year," said Pam Davy, Hostfest's executive director.

The Norsk Hostfest draws up to 60,000 people each fall, many for the Great Hall entertainment.

The four-day event at the North Dakota State Fair Center has featured big-name entertainers such as Bob Hope, Red Skelton, Alabama, Merle Haggard, Jeff Foxworthy, and the Beach Boys. The 2017 lineup includes the Oak Ridge Boys, Amy Grant, and the Doobie Brothers in the 5,000-seat Great Hall and dozens of other performers doing free shows daily from 8 a.m. to 8 p.m. on eight other stages.

The festival hosts all kinds of entertainment. There's big-time shopping for Norwegian sweaters, jewelry, Swedish clogs, Finnish saunas, and more; the Nordic Demonstration Kitchen with six chefs daily; free nightly dancing to live music; folk dancing presentations; the Author's Corner, where writers like me sit and sign their books; the Viking Village, where 70-some international actors portray Vikings doing battle and handcrafting everything from mail to jewelry; the Scandinavian Youth Camp, where kids learn Scandinavian culture through stories, dance, and making lefse; and, of course, the Lefse Masters Competition.

Masters Go for Glory

The competition began in 2015. "The idea had been bubbling in the back of my brain for a number of years," said Davy. "Lefse is so special; we all love it. It's a tradition, an addiction, *ha,* that cuts across the generations. No matter how old you are—kids, parents, grandparents—you love lefse. And lefse is a magnet; wherever there's lefse, people are immediately there. I thought it would be good to recognize and encourage the best lefse makers in the country. And once the competition came together, it was a big hit."

Home of Lefse, part of the Home of Economy discount retail chain, sponsors preliminary roll-offs each August in six North Dakota cities. Competitors may be any age, may have one assistant, and must provide their own dough and equipment. Regional winners compete in the semi-finals and, if successful, the finals at the Lefse Mezzanine in Stockholm Hall. That hall had to be rewired, by the way, said Davy, to handle all the grills needed in the competition.

On opening day of Hostfest, Wednesday, a Lefse Masters celebrity competition yields more laughs than edible lefse. When the real contest begins on Thursday, smiling spectators jam the hall to watch six lefse makers compete. Six more compete on Friday. The top four go for the title on Saturday.

As each afternoon's hour-long competition rolls on, the oh-so-satisfying smell of grilled lefse permeates the air. Flour, of course, covers the floor, the competitors' aprons, and the elevated rolling-and-grilling tables. Live music from the Stockholm Hall stage adds to the merriment.

Rolling lefse is such a cheerful event, and yet the atmosphere is charged as gray-haired and fresh-faced women, probably

accustomed to making lefse alone or in a small group, are surrounded by clutches of curious wannabes who crowd around the work tables and study every move

Lefse-making lessons are ongoing and part of the fun at the Hostfest.

the competitors make.

When time is up, competitors submit for judging one flat round, one rolled round (no toppings), and their recipes. "Some people are reluctant to turn in their recipes," said Davy, chuckling. Three chefs from Scandinavia evaluate the lefse based on appearance, taste, and texture. (Davy asked me to be a judge in 2017!) Judges award the Norsk Hostfest Lefse Masters title to the winner shortly after the competition closes. Prizes include $200, a lefse grill, gift certificates from Home of Economy, and a handcrafted, rosemaled rolling pin with the winner's name on it. The second-place

Gay Riskey, right, the 2016 Lefse Masters Competition champ, shows off her winnings. Her assistant was Zebbie Hoenke.

and third-place winners get cash ($100 for second, $50 for third) and Home of Economy gift certificates.

I'm easily influenced by lefse, but it seems to me that the Lefse Masters Competition is so unique, so joyful, and so Scandinavian that seeing it may be worth the $40 daily adult general admission to the Hostfest. After the competition ended, I only regretted that I did not get a chance to interview the 2016 Lefse Masters champ, Gay Skaflen Riskey. I also missed talking to Lefse Masters celebrity competitors Williams and Ree, who also delivered a very funny lefse bit as part of their show in Copenhagen Hall.

Fortunately, a couple of months after the Hostfest, I had a chance to interview Gay Riskey as well as Bruce Williams (see "What's So Funny About Lefse?" page 131).

Gay Riskey, Lefse Master

Coincidentally, following the Hostfest, Riskey responded to my *Viking* magazine ad calling for lefse makers to tell me their story. Considering her Scandinavian heritage, I wasn't surprised that she was rather modest about being the reigning Lefse Masters champ. Her email said: "I don't know that I would have a lot to add, but feel free to contact me. I live in North Dakota and recently competed at the Hostfest Lefse Masters Competition, taking first place."

After talking with her on the phone, I decided to drive to her home in Minto, North Dakota, to accept her invitation to see a potato harvest. I had never observed one, which seemed a shame considering potatoes are fundamental to most lefse recipes. Minto—10 miles west of the Red River of the North, 50 miles south of Canada, and three-and-a-half hours east of the hubbub of the Hostfest—is in the heart of potato country.

On a warm, late-autumn Saturday when folks were either harvesting potatoes or watching North Dakota State Bison football, Riskey had returned to earth after the high of winning the 2016 Lefse Masters Competition. One of her prizes was a lefse grill. "I have three grills now," she said, "so once I get my friends together to make lefse, we can really go to town!"

Riskey was booked to roll lefse at the Northern Plains Potato Growers Association trade show in February in Grand Forks, North Dakota. "This year, I'll make lefse to liven up the convention a little," said Riskey. "People can sample lefse and see another use of potatoes."

Tires of trucks hauling potatoes and beets throw dirt clods that turn to slippery mud in wet years.

Gay Riskey talks spuds with Nate Tallackson, a potato harvest worker near Minto, North Dakota.

I was keen on seeing potatoes being picked, so we set off on gravel roads that access the fields. Highways to the gravel roads were often lumpy with clods of soil flattened by traffic. "Those are from the tires of trucks hauling potatoes and beets," said Riskey. "The clods turn to mud in wet years, and cars can slide off the road. It's a hazard. The sheriff gets complaints, and farmers use a blade to scrape the roads. They have to clean up their mess."

We saw truck after truck loaded with potatoes and beets, but we didn't see any picking. We stopped to watch potatoes being unloaded at Quonset-type warehouses of the Associated Potato Growers, and then we returned to Minto, where Riskey showed me the $250,000 Clod Hopper 4240 potato separator. Riskey does purchasing for Harriston Industries, which manufactures the Clod Hopper.

The Clod Hopper works like this: Conveyor belts carry potatoes, soil, and stones to the top of the 4240, where small rollers separate some debris from potatoes, sending small potatoes to the front of the machine and large potatoes to the back. Two large drums in front and two in back again separate potatoes from soil and stones.

"The less dense good potatoes bounce farther off the drums and therefore separate from the denser stones and dirt clods," explained Riskey. Brilliant!

Learning how the 4240 worked may have been "inside baseball" to most, but it fascinated me—especially considering that those good potatoes might help Riskey, future Lefse Masters competitors, and many others make good lefse.

Gay Riskey stands by the $250,000 Clod Hopper 4240 potato separator.

I said goodbye to Riskey and returned home knowing I had made another good lefse friend—one of the best benefits of writing lefse books! Three months after the interview in Minto, Riskey emailed me, writing that she'd rolled lefse and offered lefse-making tips at the International Crop Expo in Grand Forks. Knowing I was always looking for tips and novel ways to serve lefse, she wrote: "One gentlemen said he dipped his in dark Karo syrup—new to me! And my coworker said her mother-in-law gave lefse with peanut butter to her sons before wrestling matches. Protein, few carbs!"

Riskey also offered the following clean-up tip:

TIP: "Clara McLean, who lived in nearby Grafton, used to line her kitchen with newspaper when making lefse. Newspapers were under her grill and all over. That made it a lot easier to clean up after making lefse. So I do that. I put newspaper under my grill and just roll it up and throw it away after I'm done."

Heritage is a big part of life. Heritage is where you come from, your values, your priorities in life. Lefse is a central part of our heritage.

—Nancy Stevenson, 65, Minot, North Dakota

Terry Ree, left, and Bruce Williams are a funny Norsk Hostfest act and an improving lefse-making team.

WHAT'S SO FUNNY ABOUT LEFSE?

Bruce Williams and Terry Ree, Lefse Masters celebrity competitors, roll for yuks on opening day of the Hostfest. When they stop goofing off and start singing and strumming, Williams and Ree are arguably the funniest, edgiest, and most talented of all the performers who consistently play the Hostfest. Lefse shows up in their act and on their CD called *Way Up Norsk.* Here is my interview with Bruce:

Legwold: *How did lefse make it into your act?*
Bruce: From working the Hostfest. I mean, we had no knowledge of lefse, per se; we had just our general experience from growing up in South Dakota and being around other people who made it. And then Pam Davy with the Hostfest put us in these lefse-making demonstrations. We learned how to roll from the resident experts, and now we can sort of do it.

Legwold: *Oh really, you make lefse?*
Bruce: We *can*. We don't, but my wife, Sharon Williams, and I have a roller and all the stuff. But we just never do it because we're not real culinary wizards.

Legwold: *So you may roll lefse at some point?*
Bruce: Yes. We may actually do that some time in our home. I doubt that Terry will ever do that because he doesn't have the equipment and he only experiences lefse while he's at the Hostfest.

Legwold: *I guarantee that once you start rolling lefse, this will only add to your comedy routine. You'll have more material.*
Bruce: At the lefse competition, we do a roll-off against one or more other performers. It usually winds up being more of a comedy routine than an actual lefse demonstration. But we're getting way, way better at it because we know some of the tricks now.

Legwold: *Give me an example of one trick you've picked up.*
Bruce: Well, keeping your flour on it at all times so the lefse doesn't stick to the roller. The first time we rolled, it was horrible. The lefse just stuck to the roller, and we weren't able to do much with it. But after you get that knowledge, you can make a pretty decent lefse.

Legwold: *Regarding your act, you're dedicating stage time for lefse, so it must mean you sense an interest there.*
Bruce: As far as our act goes, gee, we're just all over the map. We're always looking for something that will change our regular routine and involve us doing things that are out of the norm.

Legwold: *When you first did your lefse bit onstage, what was the response?*

Bruce: The response was great because at the Hostfest, it's all Scandinavian people and they get it right away. Scandinavians have a great sense of humor about their food. They almost have to because some of it is kind of gross, like lutefisk. That's pretty gross stuff. Part of the act is Terry asks who's had their lutefisk tonight. And I say you can tell because there are empty seats on both sides of those who've had their lutefisk.

Legwold: *You must be proud that you can actually get Scandinavians to laugh—out loud.*
Bruce: It's true, it's true (laughs).

Legwold: *I was at the Hostfest in 2016 and caught just a portion of your lefse bit in Copenhagen Hall.*
Bruce: That was probably a bit we had never rehearsed and had no idea about. I mean, whatever the lefse routine is on *Way Up Norsk*, it was probably a one-time deal. Whatever you hear from that point on is probably a permutation of that.

Legwold: *Comedy takes lots of preparation and is not easy at all. I'm wondering how you construct a lefse routine involving the two of you.*
Bruce: Everything we do onstage starts out as improv. We've been together almost 50 years, and when we started out, we'd get together after the show and say, "You said this and you said this, and we should try to do that again that way." But now that we're older, we just flat out can't remember what we say. So it's different every time, but that makes it funnier for us. It makes it more of a surprise when we get to laugh.

Legwold: *So with lefse, where's the humor?*
Bruce: We talk about a lot of the foods there at the Hostfest, and we sample them. When we were performing in

Oslo Hall, people brought food to the stage, and we'd sample it and talk about the consistency and flavor and grossness. That situation is tailor-made for comedy.

Legwold: *But how can you pick on lefse, such an innocent food that everybody loves?*
Bruce: (Laughs) Well, lefse is bland enough and yet universal enough that it could be used for all sorts of purposes. I mean, it's a potato thing and a flour thing, and, I don't know, in itself it's not that funny. But all the additives you put on it, you can create a routine.

Legwold: *You have this long relationship with Terry Ree, but even so, the idea of going onstage and winging it with so much improvisation seems frightening.*
Bruce: Yeah, it would be frightening for a guy like me who's not terribly improvisational, but my partner just goes on these rants and stuff, and I just interject non sequiturs—anything to interrupt his flow. That's kind of my job.

Legwold: *Last question: Do you enjoy the life of an entertainer, with all the travel and whatnot?*
Bruce: Oh, gosh, yeah. I'm not qualified to do anything else, so it's been a real boon to me. The travel is what they pay us for. Doing the gig, we'd almost do that for free—or for lefse. Will work for lefse!

14
Opheim, Montana

I don't follow a recipe. I do by feel, using potatoes, butter, half and half, salt, baking powder sometimes, and then mix it up and hope to gosh it works! The last 10 to 15 years have been pretty decent. Oh, I'll end up with a few that are more like flatbread than nice, soft lefse, but that goes with the territory.

—Janet (Larson) Spracklin, 60, Sidney, Montana

How many towns can boast that their largest employer is a lefse factory?

Only one town can also boast that the co-owner of the lefse factory was once the star of its high school girls' basketball team that won the Class C state championship three straight years (1982, '83, '84).

That town is Opheim (pop. 89 in 2014). The star of those fabled Opheim Vikings teams was Twyla Anderson, and her lefse factory is Granrud's Lefse Shack.

So it's a slam dunk that Opheim is on the Lefse Trail. This stop is the most remote and exotic, the one you'll brag about most when you complete the trail.

Granted, the protracted road trip—12 hours from Minneapolis to Opheim—will test your love of lefse. As you drive the long and unwinding two-lane roads through western North Dakota,

Twyla Anderson, once a star on Opheim's state championship basketball teams, is now co-owner of Granrud's Lefse.

you'll question the need to check off this point on the Lefse Trail. You won't pass gas stations casually in this sparsely populated country. Your misgivings about this trip will continue as you enter the northeastern corner of Big Sky Country on Montana Highway 5 and rumble through Redstone, Flaxville, and Scobey. You *know* Opheim exists because it is right there on the map, 10 miles south of the Canadian border. *But how long 'til we get there?* A town is about as common as a tree or a stream in these parts, where the prevailing view is of a big, blond ocean of wheat.

PLAINS POETRY

When driving great distances over the Great Plains, there is ample opportunity for the mind to roam and perhaps produce Plains poetry. The result may not be great poetry, but it can be fun to compose as the miles roll by. The poems on pages 137, 139, and 146 came as I journeyed west.

The visual world gets real simple here: field and sky, with sky the greater. At first you might be unnerved by this seemingly stark landscape, but as the miles roll on, you'll come to be awed by the riches: the unimpeded wash of sunlight at dawn, the changing colors of early morning, the irresistible horizon, and the various meanings of the word *vast*. Your fear of what seems to be the freakishly foreign and far-flung is replaced by fascination with the frontier. Pleasant, poetic, prayerful notions may fizz from your mind when it has a chance to float for big blocks of time in open spaces.

Lefse Is November
Blue shadows
Slanting sun
Clean fields rest
But they're not done
Faith is a circle.

Fading frost
Rising mist
Roadside grasses
Green, sun-kissed
Faith is a circle.

The grasses know
That snow is dough
Resting, rising 'til
Spring says, "It's so!"
Faith is a circle.

Yes, on the road to Opheim, you might wonder about the wisdom of such a journey. Have faith. Memories of your travels and the tour of Granrud's may make you grin the rest of your life.

The Shack

Granrud's pops up on Google as Granrud's Lefse Shack. But when my wife, Jane, and I *finally* made it to this lefse outpost just south of Opheim on Montana Highway 24, we saw a well-kept rambler with a couple of additions and three newer buildings, indicating growth of the business. The sign said Granrud's Lefse. No shack on the ground, and no *Shack* on the sign.

I asked Twyla, 49, about the lack of the shack. "Oh, shack was the idea of Myrt and Evan Granrud, the original owners who lived here," she said, grinning. "Everybody around here has called this the Lefse Shack, but we're trying to get rid of the *shack* part. Too negative."

Jane jumped right into the start of the tour. She was soon wide-eyed as she witnessed the action in the lefse-production area, a space the size of a three-stall garage. Later she would describe it as a "genius's playground." The whirl of activity brought to mind Erich Brenn's plate-spinning act on *The Ed Sullivan Show* (see You-Tube). I had to agree. I had seen rolling machines before on the Lefse Trail, but nothing like those at Granrud's.

Granrud's Lefse has supplied the Norsk Hostfest's "official" lefse for the last 40 years.

"Some people see these machines and go, 'Oh, you're cheating!'" said Twyla, over the sound of music playing on SiriusXM Radio and the thumping of four rolling pins going to and fro, nonstop. "No, we're smart. It's not really cheating because it's still rolled out. Evan made these machines so that the lefse would be as close to rolled-out by humans as possible. He knew that was the way to make good lefse."

84,000 Pounds of Potatoes

A limping Twyla led Jane and me to the potato-peeling machine. It rubs off the skins of 84,000 pounds of spuds per year. An orange rubber basketball serves as the machine's stopper. About the limp, Twyla said she farms and ranches when not running Granrud's, and a heifer going to market "charged me and got me

Twyla Anderson, left, and Alice Redfield used to manage Granrud's but then became co-owners in 2005.

good. Farming and ranching work slows down now [late October], so lefse is a good winter thing."

Workers remove the eyes of peeled potatoes and then cut up the potatoes for cooking. Potatoes boil for 25 to 30 minutes in four canners at once. Many days, said Twyla, the crew does 16 canners, which is about 1,000 pounds of potatoes. When the potatoes are done, the entire stage of burners beneath the canners tips forward and water drains from the canners through black hoses running to a five-gallon bucket. This automated draining protects against back strain as workers dump potatoes into a large steel mixing bowl.

Cream, milk, margarine, salt, and sugar are added to the potatoes by hand. No preservatives are added, although there is a preservative (vitamin A palmitate) in the margarine. The mixer produces a well-beaten dough that is scooped by hand into six-quart tubs. The tubs are left to cool for about an hour to room temperature and then chilled further in a walk-in cooler. Prolonged cooling is key to tasty lefse, according to the folks at Granrud's. "That's kinda what makes the lefse good," said co-owner Alice Redfield, 58. "The dough needs time for rest and for the ingredients to mix.

Morning in Montana

The sky arches as a monstrous
question mark:
Why?
I don't know, so
I ask a grouse
  It isn't pleased
I ask a hawk
  It simply balks
I ask an owl
  It glares and scowls
I ask the wheat
  It waves to greet
I ask the grass
  It says, "I'll pass."
I ask a boy
  He says, "Enjoy."
So I surrender. Turn it over.
Let it go.
With winter looming,
I face east, smile into the morning
  See the milkweed's seed
  Hear the backlit strands of silk
  Singing in parts
Why?
Why not?

A potato-peeling machine rubs off skins of 84,000 pounds of spuds yearly. A rubber basketball is the machine's stopper.

The entire stage of burners beneath the canners tips forward to drain potato-boiling water, thus saving manual labor.

Evan came up with that, maybe by accident. But we keep on doing what he started."

After sufficient cooling (it's Granrud's secret how long), dough and flour are mixed by machine. "We use about 300 pounds of flour a day, and with rolling, about half of it ends up on the floor," said Twyla.

The dough-flour mixture is then hand-packed into 2-foot-long tubes about the width of a gallon paint can. "You gotta really stuff the dough in there to make sure there are no air pockets," said Alice. Once the tubes are packed, it's rolling time.

A DIYer's Delight

The tube is just one example of a common Montana man showing uncommon moxie and ambition: Evan Granrud devised a remarkable system by himself. To understand how his invention works, picture one operator sitting in a "cockpit." The packed tube is on her left. She steps on the tube's pedal, which causes a pneumatic plate to push up from the bottom so that ¼ inch of dough pops above the tube's top rim. The operator rotates a steel arm

Jeremy Foster scoops lefse dough into six-quart tubs that are cooled before rolling.

After flour is added to cooled dough, co-owner Alice Redfield firmly packs dough into a tube that holds enough to make 65 lefse rounds.

that looks like a hacksaw with a thin, taut wire in place of a blade. The wire slices off this protruding ¼ inch of dough, thus creating a patty. The tube holds enough dough to make 65 patties.

The operator feeds patties to two machines relentlessly rolling lefse. For each machine, she transfers a patty to one of three cloth-covered, circular, rotating pastry boards. As the machine rolls one patty on one board, the operator slices off another patty from the tube and centers it on an empty board. When the patty is rolled out to the size of a dinner plate, that board automatically rotates from under the rolling pin. Thus, by constantly slicing patties and feeding them to the six rotating boards, the operator does a lefse-maker's version of a spinning-plates act.

The way these pastry boards rotate in coordination with the rolling machine is brilliant. The boards are millimeters beneath a grooved, sock-covered rolling pin. A tray drops flour onto spinning paint rollers that then dust flour onto the rolling pin. Flour, of course, prevents the patty from sticking to the heavy rolling pin.

When a pastry board bearing a patty rotates to a position beneath the rolling pin, the board is automatically pushed up so the patty contacts the pin. The pressure between pin and patty has to be just right—too much pressure and the patty squishes and sticks; too little pressure and rolling the round takes too long.

When the pin rolls over the patty and beyond the patty's edge, the pin is still pressing on the board. Therefore, the board must move lower so that it can turn freely. This board turning ensures that the patty ends up as round, not oblong, lefse. Once the board turns, it moves back up to contact position, and the pin makes a return pass.

Thus, the board pistons up, and the pin rolls across and beyond the patty. The board moves down, then turns. Board up, pin rolls over and past the patty. Board down, board turns. And on and on, until the machine senses the patty is fully rolled.

How does the machine know when the patty is rolled to the desired size? Mounted on the rolling machine's frame is what Twyla called "a computer eye" that shines a blue light down on the board about 2 inches in from the edge. "As soon as the lefse is rolled out to that point, the computer eye senses the round is done and signals the machine to rotate the table," said Twyla.

"We bought the computer eye in 2005," said Alice. "It can tell the difference between the color of the lefse and the color of the table. Before the computer eye, a worker had to use a pedal to rotate the table when the round was done. So there was one worker at each machine."

"Finding workers, especially near Opheim, is a problem," said Twyla. "But with this computer eye, we are able to sit one person at two machines. And the rolling goes

Mary Honrud steps on a pedal that pushes dough up ¼ inch. She swings the steel arm that holds a wire which cuts a patty. Granrud's lefse-rolling machine rolls the patty into a round.

Patties are centered on boards that automatically rotate under constantly moving rolling machines.

faster because before the computer eye, you know, people would be talking and wouldn't push the pedal. Well, the board automatically rotates now."

Cooling Is Cool

Once the machine has rolled a round to the desired size, one of the two grillers uses a lefse stick to lift the round onto a 350-degree gas grill made of ¾-inch steel. After cooking both sides, the griller sends the round on a 5-minute journey on a cooling conveyor. The conveyor consists of five 8-foot lengths of belts stacked and offset from each other. Fans blow on hot lefse as it first moves one direction on the top belt and then drops to the belt below, which moves in the opposite direction. In this fashion, lefse cools on three more belts and then drops to a pickup table.

The pickup table—an angled 4-foot-wide, vinyl-covered turn-table—catches the cooled lefse rounds, which drop to the lower side. As the table rotates, the rounds rise to the waist level of a worker, who stacks them on a small table and cuts some into halves or quarters. The worker packages the lefse as whole, half, or quarter rounds. Each plastic bag contains 1 pound of lefse.

A worker puts the packages on trays, and the lefse further cools at room temperature. Then packages are placed on racks and rolled into a freezer. Granrud's makes about 560 packages daily and 55,000 packages a year. Once frozen, the lefse is boxed and sealed, 16 packages in a box, for shipping to retailers and individual customers in all 50 states.

Official Lefse of Norsk Hostfest

Widespread demand is a testament to how good Granrud's lefse is. It's not by chance that Granrud's has been the Norsk Hostfest's "official" lefse for the last 40 years.

"Usually we send out email reminders to customers during lefse season, but we didn't do it last year because of the possibility that we were not going to be able to fill the order," said Twyla. "Finally we had to stop taking orders because we ran out of lefse in the middle of December. Last year we were so short on staff. It was crazy. One side of the production room or the other wasn't going, which cut production in half.

"We could sell more if we advertised. All these snowbirds move to Arizona, where they can't buy lefse. And on the East Coast, they can't get lefse there. There's a market out there. Somebody could make a lot of money because there's a lot of people out there who want lefse."

Anyone with concerns about the future of lefse has to like hearing that!

Lefse makers are usually rewarded for making good lefse, but in one case Granrud's lefse was too good. For a few years, Granrud's made lefse for a Lutheran church event, which also sold lefse made by church members. However, one year Granrud's

A "computer eye" senses when a round is rolled to the desired width and signals the lefse-rolling machine to rotate the board.

was asked not to come back because Granrud's lefse was outselling member-made lefse. "But then there were complaints that we were not there," said Alice, laughing, "and we were asked back again the following year.

"It's funny, customers tell us our lefse is as good as what their mom makes—but they'll whisper, 'Don't tell my mom that.'"

After patties are rolled to the desired width, Tom Schwartz transfers each round to the grill.

No, I do not have a tip on making perfect rounds. I remember my mom joking, "Well, let's see ... this one looks like Africa." I get the same shapes. I don't worry about perfect lefse. They all taste the same.

—Janet (Larson) Spracklin, 60, Sidney, Montana

PRONOUNCING *OPHEIM*

Montana pulls you west because its open spaces offer optimism. "I can do it in Montana," should be the state's motto, not *Oro y Plata,* Spanish for Gold and Silver.

Say you have a hankering to have a town named after you. You can do it in Montana, even if you have no claim to fame. Opheim was established in 1911 and named after Alfred

Sumner Opheim (1872–1949), who was the town's *second* postmaster; his wife, Helen (Ouandahl) Opheim (1874–1930), was the first. So there you go: In Montana, even if you are the second postmaster in the town's history, you can have a town named after you. That is, if you are a man. If you are the first postmaster and a woman, you are not likely to have the town named after you anywhere. As a married woman, you probably gave up your original surname altogether. Maybe not even your first name will be engraved on the headstone you share with your husband. Women easily disappear from history.

Now, if you do get a town named after you, you want visitors to get the name right, right? But that's not easy with a name like Opheim. In fact, going down the list of 128 Montana cities and towns, Opheim is the easiest to mispronounce, in my humble opinion. You'll probably pick up the proper pronunciation when touring Granrud's Lefse in Opheim. In case you don't, I offer the following:

Lefse Helps You Learn
I betcha a dime
You'll misstate Opheim
So in I will chime:

If you say O-Feem,
Residents will scream.
If your first sound is Oph,
You'll be seen as an oaf.
So go with an O
And end with a Pime.
Sublime!

Just remember:
In Opheim
It's lefse time
All the time.

CREDIT THE RACCOONS

Evan Granrud had worked at the U.S. Air Force base in Glasgow, Montana, before it closed in the 1970s, sung in a bar in Glentana, raised chickens, worked at mudding and taping sheetrock, and held a job setting up satellite dishes. In the mid-1970s in Opheim, Montana, Myrt Granrud, Evan's spouse, started making lefse for a Lutheran church event and selling it at the Good News bookstore. Word spread, and Granrud's Lefse began in 1977. And Myrt got swamped.

"They had a crew rolling it and rolling it," said Twyla Anderson, Granrud's co-owner, "and they were up until all hours of the night."

The crew didn't have enough refrigerators and freezers to store all the lefse, so they put packages on top of freezers in the open walkway between the house and the garage. "One morning, after they'd worked until midnight making lefse," said Twyla, "they got up and lefse was spread all over the yard. The raccoons had gotten into the packages."

Even after Evan pitched in with rolling and grilling, Granrud's still could not keep up with demand. "Finally, Evan said this isn't going to work; we just need to make it faster," said Twyla. "He decided he was going to make a machine to roll lefse that was as close to hand-rolled as it could possibly get. The women told him he couldn't do it."

He proved them wrong, but he had to fail in order to succeed. "This is about the third prototype that we're using now," said Twyla.

Myrt and Evan, who have passed on, grew the business and then sold it in 1997 to the Rural Electric Company. Eight years later, REC sold to Alice Redfield and Twyla. "By the time we bought it, REC was ready to get rid of it," said Twyla. "We managed it. We were doing all the work, and we said, 'We should buy this place.'"

"They didn't have the time and didn't want to make all the decisions needed to run this place," said Alice. "They gave us the lowest interest rate and worked with us. We paid $165,000 over 10 years, and we just paid it off in 2015."

"So your investment means Granrud's is here to stay?" I asked.

"I don't know how long we'll be here," said Twyla. "There are not many local workers. That's our main challenge."

Granrud's employs eight workers, but as with all lefse factories, finding help is an ongoing problem. The crew includes a Chicago woman and a man from Long Prairie, Minnesota, who saw a Granrud's Craigslist ad. The ad offered employees free rent in the rambler that adjoins the lefse factory. In exchange for free rent, the employees must clean the factory on weekends.

(Here's an idea: Granrud's could offer lefse-making internships or residencies to students of culinary arts for the fall semester.)

"We're not getting any younger," said Twyla. "It's hard work with all the lifting and everything. So it's probably going to be sooner rather than later that we make a move. I don't know. I've had talks with a guy out of Great Falls, Montana. He could raise the capital in a day. But I don't know if we'd sell. Maybe we'd just get investors and rebuild it bigger somewhere else, a place where there's more of a workforce."

Evan and Myrt Granrud started Granrud's Lefse in 1977. High demand forced Evan to invent ingenious lefse-rolling machines.

15
Portland, Oregon

You just practice. That's all part of making a round lefse. So many of my lefse in the early years looked like the Scandinavian peninsula or Iceland. Or they'd have a hole, like somebody put one of the Great Lakes in the middle of my lefse.

—Bill Wilson, 69, Scotts Mills, Oregon

I gleefully groaned when I heard of Viking Soul Food—the world's first and only lefse-wrap food truck. The glee was in the notion of such a food truck. What a hoot! I *had* to see this thing and taste the lefse wraps. The groan was in the distance. When I learned Viking Soul Food was in Portland, Oregon, far from my home in Minnesota, I scratched my head and asked: "Cute idea,

Inside this 18-foot 1958 Streamline trailer, Viking Soul Food's chefs create delectable lefse wraps.

but is such a far-flung food truck really worthy of inclusion on the Lefse Trail?"

Yabetcha!

This is the trail's "lefse-plus" stop. You get lefse plus gourmet food. I could almost say the mouthwatering morsels in the wraps make the lefse secondary. But that would be a stretch. Lefse doesn't take a back seat to any food! It's just that the wraps are filled with all sorts of wonderfully seasoned stuff that floods your senses. Your eyes roll. You drool. You moan. You must sit and take a moment, to be one with this wrap, to study its size, and to project how long you'll remain in this ecstasy. At Viking Soul Food, you can taste fresh lefse and feel its velvety texture on your tongue, but lefse is not the soloist; it is the cornerstone singer in a toe-tapping octet. The end result is music for the mouth, Viking soul music.

Lefse Pride

I was never prouder of lefse than when I was at Viking Soul Food. Lefse stood tall before strangers. In the context of a food truck serving the masses in an urban mix of cultures, lefse graciously reached out to bring non-Scandinavians into the fold.

The trip confirmed that lefse performs well no matter the stage. I was delighted by the way lefse played to Portland people of all ages. They often didn't know lefse from rightse. And before tasting the soft flatbread, they may have been skeptical: Was lefse a Norwegian no-flavor knockoff tortilla?

Lefse was being tested outside the Midwest's Scandinavian lefse sanctuary, and it won over skeptics with one bite. A lefse wrap is the best kind of wrap. Period. Lefse brings something more to the party than the ability to contain other delicacies. Unlike other wraps that have all the appeal of good food enveloped in plastic, Viking Soul Food wraps offer a soft, floury feel; a lively, leopard-skin look; and a toasty, potato-y tang. I repeat: A lefse wrap is the best kind of wrap.

Epicurean Delights

I flew to Portland the night before my meeting with Viking Soul Food owners Megan Walhood, 41, and Jeremy Daniels, 33. I awoke to a wet-but-clearing October morn, and I hopped on the MAX Red Line light rail. I departed at the Hollywood Transit Center, took a bus to Belmont Street, and walked to The Bite on Belmont, a food-truck park in southeast Portland.

Ten food trucks were jammed into The Bite. Each had its specialty (Brazilian, Korean-Hawaiian, Mediterranean, Mexican, Scandinavian, Thai, fish, mac and cheese, beer, coffee).

At the back end of The Bite, I found Megan inside a rounded, polished 18-foot 1958 Streamline with a flat tire. She was thumping out round after round of lefse. When she and Jeremy started Viking Soul Food in 2010, Megan named the Streamline Gudrun. "Gudrun was one of the Valkyries," said Megan, "one of Odin's 12 handmaidens who conducted slain warriors from the battlefield to Valhalla."

Outside, Gudrun had an orange umbrella above the ordering window and a blackboard displaying a menu of tempting wraps,

Viking Soul Food co-owner Megan Walhood says they make 50 to 150 lefse each day, depending on the season.

as well as side dishes, snacks, and drinks. *Vanquishing Mediocrity Since 2010* was handwritten at the top of the blackboard. In the middle of the menu, the words *Conquering the Generic* appeared above a photo of lefse on a grill. Some menu items change as Megan and Jeremy see fit, but that day the list of options included these four meals, all wrapped in freshly made lefse:

- Norwegian meatballs in caramelized goat cheese (gjetost) gravy with sweet-and-sour cabbage
- House-smoked salmon, dill crème fraîche, pickled shallots, mixed lettuces, and green cabbage
- Pølse (Swedish potato sausage), Jarlsberg cheese, mustard, lingonberries, surkål (sour cabbage), and tangy slaw
- Vegetarian combo of house recipe mushroom and hazelnut patties, blue cheese, parsley sauce, and mixed lettuces

Snacks included herring in wine sauce, a pickled hard-boiled egg with black pepper mayo and caviar, house-cured thick-cut bacon, and the Troll Snack of roasted garlic and Jarlsberg cheese spread on a rye crisp.

For dessert, these sweet lefse wraps were listed:
• Lingonberries and house cream cheese
• Lemon curd and spiced pecans
• Roasted Washington apples, chèvre, walnuts, and sherry syrup

Also offered were rounds of lefse with butter and cane sugar or butter and local honey as well as lingonberry iced tea. Prices ranged from $3 for buttered rounds to $8.50 for dinner wraps.

Only superlative discipline prevented me from scrapping the interview and eating my way through this menu. That and it was only 10 a.m. and the food was still being prepared for the noon opening. After the interview, I did consume—for research purposes—the lefse wrap of Norwegian meatballs in gjetost gravy with sweet-and-sour cabbage. Megan said it was their best seller. As I relished the lefse wrap with a glass of lingonberry iced tea, I heard Viking soul music!

But back to the interview. While Megan rolled lefse and Jeremy prepped the stuffings as well as rolled, I asked questions and danced around them inside the Gudrun, which has about twice as much workspace as a commercial airplane kitchen. This fascinating conversation showed me how this refreshing couple pulls off preparing food that successfully walks the line between honoring tradition and being sassy.

Legwold: How do you make your lefse, and how many rounds do you make each day?
Megan: We weigh on a digital scale each dough ball at 3 ounces. We roll it out, and each lefse cooks 40 seconds a side. While one side bakes, we roll out another round. We don't use a sock on our rolling pins. Flour fills the grooves, and Jeremy feels grooves serve to lay flour on the lefse. I just never bother to put a sock on the pin.
Jeremy: We have to replace pastry boards a lot because the feet come off. I mean, these things get hammered pretty hard. The grills last about two years. The feet break. The electrical breaks.
Megan: We make 50 to 60 rounds a day this time of year [fall]. In the summer, it's 100 to 150. At Christmastime, obviously, we're making as much as possible (laughs). We have three employees,

so it's not just Jeremy and me rolling. Teresa Snelling, for example, is our lefse superstar. In the weeks leading up to Christmas, these grills will probably be going all the time. Lots of people can make lefse, but can they make it fast enough? It's all about speed. If you're not fast enough over here [at the board], your lefse is going to overcook over here [at the grill].

Megan and Jeremy prep for the lunchtime opening. The trailer, aka the Gudrun, has about twice as much workspace as a commercial airplane kitchen.

Legwold: How is your lefse recipe different from other recipes?

Megan: We make the dough the night before, and the dough is mashed potatoes and olive oil. We don't use butter and cream because we want dairy-free lefse for people who have allergies or are vegan. We also found we like the texture better. When the dough is cold, with olive oil it's not quite as firm as it would be if it were butter; butter has saturated fat and congeals more at colder temperatures than olive oil. Our recipe is potatoes, olive oil, and salt. No sugar. We want the lefse to be more neutral. My grandmother's recipe had a tiny amount of sugar in it. But I ended up omitting sugar to keep the lefse neutral, a versatile platform for whatever we're going to put on it. The end result is it works well with savory things and sweet things.

Jeremy: People love our lefse with the olive oil. We did a taste test with the family, and they liked it. The olive oil adds a floral, fruity element.

Megan: We don't want rounds to be super done; we want them to be almost underdone. We toast them a second time on the grill, right before serving. Toast the lefse too much and it gets tough. If you don't toast the round quite long enough, it can tear when you roll the ingredients inside. When you toast them a second time, you want to wait until you see them bubble up a bit, like this. ... When we first roll out the lefse, we take pains to dust off the flour. If we left the flour on, the flour might then burn when we toast them. We don't want burnt flour.

Jeremy: Megan trained me to make lefse, and it was an intense month—very intense month (laughs). It was fun, though. It was intense because she grew up making it and it was so important to her—and to all the customers who've come to visit and told us just how good it needed to be. I needed to roll it just so. The amount of pressure on the rolling pin, the look—things needed to be just so. I needed to flip it just so. Everything needed to be super spot-on. Intense. She made sure that everything went over just right. Because of that, though—and we're still together after 10 years—we have very good lefse and I'm able to train people pretty well.

Legwold: Since you are using the lefse for a wrap, you don't need perfectly round lefse, do you?

Megan: Because we are using the lefse like a tortilla and wrapping stuff in it, we just want relative uniformity so it's easy to deal with.

Jeremy: When I was learning, Megan wouldn't accept anything less than perfection. My training method with the employees is a little bit different. It's like, "Let's shoot for perfection. Let's shoot for as even as possible and as circular as possible, but when it doesn't happen? Totally fine." That's how it always happens. But if you make a perfectly circular one and the thickness is just so—which happens like two times a year—be very happy about that. Always shoot for it. Never expect it to happen.

Legwold: I see on your website that you ship lefse.

Megan: People wanted us to ship, but we've never done it because we just couldn't stand by the quality of the product. But we experimented last year and froze small packages of six rounds. We found that the rounds thaw out nicely and stay really soft and

One smoked salmon lefse wrap coming up!

supple. Shipping lefse is an add-on, and the challenge is keeping up with that kind of production on top of the food-truck business. Initially, our whole mission was to see if people would even buy lefse wraps at all. Well, it totally works. People love it, and the fun thing is we get to expose people to lefse who have never even heard of it. A good portion of our customers are Scandinavian, but a lot of them are just people from the neighborhood who tried it and fell in love with it.

Legwold: *I love the name "Viking Soul Food." How did you get started with this lefse-wrap food-truck idea?*
Megan: The Viking Soul Food was a play on words. I came up with the name and was thinking what lefse means to a lot of people, and what a comfort food it is. It's sort of like soul food for Scandinavians. We've done food that is traditional. We didn't mess around with the gjetost-meatball recipe much, for example. But we wanted a vegan wrap that was really good, so we created these mushroom-and-hazelnut patties. We serve those with blue cheese and parsley sauce. Our recipes are based on research of Scandinavian recipes, but they are mostly our creation.

Our hot sauce that goes with the gjetost-meatball wrap is totally untraditional, except that it uses beets. All in all, we wanted to have respect for the tradition, but we also wanted to be irreverent and have fun with things. And that's what we did.

Legwold: How did you two combine forces to form Viking Soul Food?
Megan: We're both chefs by trade and met cooking at a local restaurant called Nostrana. We developed a style of cooking together and did supper club dinners. We really wanted to start something together and get our food out there. Originally, we thought about something to do with Jeremy's family heritage, which is more Pacific Island. So we were thinking about Pacific Island food or Polynesian, and, while that is unique, we wanted to do something that was *very* unique. In the latter part of 2009, we started thinking about doing something with Norwegian meatballs and lefse.

Legwold: Why Norwegian meatballs and lefse?
Jeremy: At a gathering of Megan's family, I was getting talked at for how much I was standing in the kitchen and just eating all the lefse and the meatballs. This was the first time I had experienced these things, and it was so exciting for me—the culture and the food. I'm very food obsessed, so I was in the kitchen and just eating, eating, eating.

Legwold: You had never eaten lefse before then? What did you think?
Jeremy: When I first experienced lefse, it was such a transformative, really spectacular experience. When I tasted it, it seemed like I could have or should have been eating it since I was a little kid. It was so comforting. It was beautiful. Beautiful! So that was it for me. I just ate it plain, right off the grill. Eating the lefse, eating the meatballs. And Megan said, "Hey, you have to come talk at some point here. You can't just stay in the kitchen and eat." This was the first time I had met the family, and they were wondering, "Who is the guy just standing and eating in the kitchen?"
Megan: So he decided to combine the lefse and meatballs and go mingle. And everyone in my family said, "What did you do?" Really! He was the originator of our concept of putting meat-

balls inside of lefse. I don't know if I would have thought to do that. His brain works differently. He'll have an idea that's crazy, and I'll temper it. But we come up with something usable. He's probably brought the more open mind about how things could be done. Partly, it's a function of my obsessive personality. But also coming from my Norwegian culture, I definitely felt that, "Oh, no, it has to be like this because that's how it's always been done." He's not carrying any of that baggage, so he can say, "Well, we can try it like this and see what happens." I definitely had my moments when he had to convince me.

Legwold: How did you go from original lefse-wrap recipes to setting up a food-truck business?
Megan: As far as setting up the business, the barriers to entry were low, especially in Portland, where you're allowed to park somewhere and just stay there. You don't have to move every four hours. In Portland, you just find what they call a food cart pod, and you can hang out there. You sign a lease and pay rent and hang out there. A lot of people still choose the mobile thing and, for example, go to Nike and sell lunches. We were able to get this whole thing started for less that $15,000. The 1958 trailer was the biggest expense, about $6,700. Then the equipment like that kitchen grill was a pretty big expense, along with insurance and startup odds and ends.

Legwold: I like that lefse is fundamental to your food, not just served with one or two items on the menu.
Megan: The foundational dish, the lefse wrap with meatballs and gjetost sauce, was a way to expose people to lefse, people who are into the food-cart and casual fast-food scene. Also, as many Scandinavians as there are in this country, there are still a lot of people who just don't know what lefse is. We want them to know, but it isn't easy. There was a time after we got started that we realized how much work making lefse is. If we were just using a pre-made tortilla, it would be so easy. But the texture of lefse and its toasty potato flavor is so special.
Jeremy: A big part of Megan's growing up was rolling lefse with her dad, Dale Walhood, who was originally from Devils Lake,

Savor this lunch of lingonberry iced tea and a lefse wrap of Norwegian meatballs in gjetost gravy with sweet-and-sour cabbage.

North Dakota. Sadly, he and her mother, Patricia Mae Mathews Walhood, recently passed on. We wanted to do something that honored her heritage. I wanted to take the opportunity to get into her culture, and Megan knew only a little about Norwegian food. So we wanted to learn more but not have these stereotypes. We came up with the concept of the lefse wrap, and then we decided we could do this, expose people to this thing.

Megan: You gotta keep things fresh. If you want to get a younger generation excited about it, you have to make lefse seem cool.

Jeremy: I'm a good example. I think it's very cool. Touching back on that first experience I had with lefse, where I felt that I should have always been eating lefse, it just felt that way. I think if you expose people to this product and show them that it's this cool combination between a tortilla and a crepe made with mashed potatoes, and a really beautiful product, folks can get on board.

Legwold: Did you do any marketing in the beginning?

Megan: We just opened and hoped for the best. We got good press from a local food blogger, Jen Stevenson, who has a book [called] *Portland's 100 Best Places to Stuff Your Faces.*

Co-owner Jeremy Daniels: "When I first experienced lefse, it ... seemed like I could have or should have been eating it since I was a little kid. It was so comforting. It was beautiful. Beautiful!"

Jeremy: We were younger chefs and really wanted to make our mark, so it was an ego-driven thing. We really wanted to make a splash. It was our full intention to get our names out there and see what we could do, to prove it not only to other people but also to ourselves. After we'd been going a couple years, we wanted to make this sustainable instead of just feeding our ego. So we started training other people, and we've come up with standardized recipes that workers can follow.

Legwold: I love the idea of taking lefse to the streets and seeing how it is received. What has been the general public's response to lefse?
Megan: For people who have not heard of lefse, it's, "Oh, this is a totally new thing." But the interesting thing is they assume this is a common street food in Norway. It's not. Then you have people who are familiar with lefse. Sometimes they're excited about it, and they think it's cool. Sometimes they're skeptical—even a little scandalized that we would serve lefse with something besides butter and sugar. It's like, "Really?" Of course, people are very proud about their lefse or their grandmother's lefse, and

they come here and don't expect the lefse to be good. Or they assume that there's no way we're making our own lefse and that we must be buying Mrs. Olson's or something. I think they assume that because they know how much work it is, and they can't imagine anyone would be this insane to make fresh lefse every day. And it is a fair point—it is insane! (laughs) So a lot of people come skeptical to the ordering window. Then they try our lefse and are not skeptical anymore.

Legwold: I also love that you are a biracial couple and out front on the lefse scene. My daughter is Colombian, and my grandkids are Colombian and black. I am relieved that they have embraced lefse, and lefse has embraced them. But Jeremy, how has it been serving lefse and lefse wraps when you are perceived as being non-Scandinavian?
Jeremy: Overall positive. However, especially at the beginning, we had a few occasions when folks would come to the Gudrun to order: They looked Scandinavian and were checking out the menu, very excited. I was out of view. When they came to the window to order, I came to the window. They all kind of turn toward each other and whispered—and they walked away. That doesn't happen much, but it's happened a few times. It's shocking because I was thinking, "I can still make the food. I promise, it's good. My wife trained me so hard, it's going to be great. You'll love it!" But they didn't want to give it a chance. And that's the bummer part. Yes, I wanted their business, but I also wanted to expose them to this food because it was going to be good. And then there are other people, Scandinavians, who come to the window, and they see me in the window. They say in a totally nonoffensive way, "You don't look Norwegian!" Or "What part of Scandinavia are you from?"

Legwold: What is your ethnic background?
Jeremy: Korean, Chinese, Spanish, black, Filipino, and Cherokee.
Megan: And I'm Norwegian. It's been kind of hard not to get upset sometimes, when I feel like people are being racially offensive. There have been those very few times when we were working and people were so turned off by his skin color that they

didn't eat here. I didn't think we lived in that world anymore. So I was like, "Wow, there are people who are still like that!" I've struggled with it a little bit because I've felt really protective of him; I do not want people to think that way or assume that only someone with 100-percent Norwegian blood can make lefse. That 100-percent Norwegian blood is a myth, anyway. I try to have a sense of humor about it. I feel like we've had positive experiences, and it's getting better. Most people do not mean anything by it. Most people are just proud of their heritage. When we started out, they may have felt their culture had been so underrepresented and if someone was going to represent it, they'd better do it right. That may be why we had people at first say, "So, what are you guys doing?"

Legwold: Have you felt accepted by the Scandinavian community?
Jeremy: In those first couple years, it was a little more difficult. It was not like people were threatening us or anything. But it seemed kind of odd that we weren't fully welcomed into the community.
Megan: You know where it was really noticeable was at Scandinavian festivals. I've had festival people putting me front and center, and he's hiding in the back. People at the festivals would see him standing in a booth. They'd never seen him before, and they didn't know what Viking Soul Food was—and here was a brown person. They'd just walk past.
Jeremy: They were not going to take the food seriously. I have this charismatic and joyful thing about me. I just like being happy and sharing that. It was hard for me at first when some people weren't accepting me. We'd go to festivals and people would excitedly say, "Hey, Megan!" And I'm right next to her.
Megan: He's gotten more accepted as the years have gone by. And for some of them, they don't know very many brown people. Now it's kind of a point of pride for them, that they have grown to accept him.

Legwold: Jeremy, I'm sure you've rolled lefse and had people watching your every move.
Jeremy: Yeah. Megan has lots of uncles, and they are the Lefse

Commission. I have been accepted, but I had to prove my mettle by looking competent while making it—and it had to taste good. Their praise was actually high praise for Norwegians: a shrug, a ho-hum, and a "pretty good."

Megan: His family was totally fine with the mixed couple thing. He's from Hawaii, which is so mixed. For my parents, it was not a problem at all. When my grandfather Cyrus Walhood moved here in the 1950s from North Dakota, he went into business with a black

Viking Soul Food's lefse recipe calls for mashed potatoes and olive oil.

guy. I don't know why, but they became friends and a lot of people thought he was crazy. My dad was a school psychologist in Vancouver, Washington, and that helped with being understanding and open. My mom was a school librarian in the Portland public school system in northeast Portland, which is mostly black. I was in the minority in class.

Legwold: In your own way and in your own little corner of the world, you are using lefse to move the needle with race relations.
Megan: Which is a powerful way to do that because people really connect through food. It's gratifying to think that we might be breaking down some people's unconscious biases and preconceived notions—and opening people's minds.

Lefse-making is the sharing of love.

–Lou Ann Thorsness, 60, Salem, Oregon

Astrid Blackwell, left, and Barbara Overen Smith roll lefse. Barbara: "I don't even like to eat lefse as much as I like to make it."

HOPE THE MAIL BEATS THE MOLD

You can't rush lefse. That's the thought I had during my interview with Barbara Overen Smith, 76, of Bend, Oregon. We must have talked lefse for an hour and a half. Her low-keyed voice and methodical explanations made for easy listening. She shared the following gems of lefse-making wisdom and tips:

I don't even like to eat lefse as much as I like to make it. I just think it's fun. And then to share my heritage. People with Scandinavian ancestry or who grew up around Scandinavians have recollections from their childhood of the smell of burnt flour and hot-off-the-griddle lefse. If we can use lefse to keep that heritage going through the generations, that's a wonderful way to keep pride in our heritage.

TIP: If you get a slight tear or hole, overlap your lefse at the tear–or place a small piece of dough over the hole–then tamp the ends together lightly. Roll back and forth over the spot gently a few times, then turn the lefse and continue. This should mend the hole. It works early in the rolling, but not so well when the round is almost done.

My mother, Olga Johnson Overen, would make a small log of lefse dough and put it on the back of the counter; this she called "letting it rest." She'd sit and have a cup of coffee, and then she would get up and roll this out, making about eight lefse. She'd repeat the whole process of making dough until the 10 pounds of potatoes were used up. Then she would start over with boiling another 10 pounds of potatoes for the next day. She was doing this while my boys were in school and I was at work.

TIP: Put your big potatoes on the bottom of a cooking pot and small potatoes on top. Cover with water, unsalted. Bring to a boil. Lower the temperature to a slow boil or simmer for approximately 20 minutes until done. Potatoes are done when a long wire or fork goes into a potato easily, without breaking the potato apart. Overcooking can cause potatoes to pop open and be wet and mushy.

TIP: Lefse will keep OK for a week or so refrigerated; keeping it longer means you should freeze it. When refrigerating or freezing, make sure the lefse is cold before sealing the bag. If the lefse is not cold, moisture will form in the bag. To prevent moisture, put a paper towel on top of the lefse until the vapor ceases to form in the bag. Then remove the paper towel.

My mother would wrap up one dozen or two dozen lefse at a time and put them in the freezer. When she had enough done, hopefully in time for Christmas, I was called on to help wrap them for shipping and rush them to the post office. I vividly recall standing in the freezing-cold weather, waiting my turn to get to the door of a small trailer on East Main Street–this was the UPS in Klamath Falls, Oregon. The hope was the lefse would get to its destination before it turned green from mold–and also by Christmas Eve.

Part 2
Learning to Get a Round

16
The Lefse Revolution!

I've been making lefse for about 40 years, and no matter what I do, it's my nature to always try to improve the way I've done it. I want to make lefse as exact or as nice-looking as possible.

—Barbara Overen Smith, 76, Bend, Oregon

When I *finally* learned to make a respectable round of lefse, I was relieved ... and then elated. I was relieved because this was after years of thrashing about in a quicksand of flour and failure. Linda Bengtson (see Chapter 1) threw a lifeline and yanked me out of the lefse messes I had created each Thanksgiving. She offered her recipe. She passed on tons of tips. She assured and affirmed, and reassured and reaffirmed. And yet, I was *still* botching each batch—until she happed to ask: "What kind of pastry cloth do you use?"

I frowned. "Pastry cloth? What's a pastry cloth?"

I didn't know pastry cloth from pastrami. But I learned, and that was the last piece of the puzzle. I was out of the quicksand and on the firm shores of Lefse Land. I was more than an eater; I was a lefse maker. Me! I made lots of lefse and was in the club that included Grandma Jennie Legwold. I could bring amazing lefse (redundancy?) to holiday events, and friends and family would *ooh!* and *aah!* and gush ecstatically.

Buoyed by such support and adulation, I wanted to keep it going. Don't mess with success, right? So I became fixed, almost superstitiously, to Linda's recipe and my rituals. I taught them to friends and students in my lefse-making classes. I would never admit it, but I came to believe there was only one way to make lefse, at least lefse that was any good. I had to make it the way Linda made it. Her recipe became chiseled in stone, and I would lug the LEFSE RECIPE tablets down from the mountaintop and prayerfully present them in my kitchen to my awestruck students.

My lefse-making successes supported my certainty. In my little world, I became the go-to person regarding all things lefse. Linda crowned me Lefse King because she didn't want the Lefse Queen job anymore. Sometimes greatness is thrust upon you, right? I wrote a *Minnesota Monthly* article about learning to make lefse. That well-received piece led to writing *The Last Word on Lefse,* which included stories, recipes, and a how-to section.

Refinement

Other lefse makers have humbled me. They have taught me that there are lots of ways to make lefse—very good lefse. Every one of them has passed on something useful—rubber bands to hold the rolling-pin sock in place, blocks under the rolling table to prevent stooping. Their advice could help me become a little better at making lefse and keep on rolling for years.

I can link arms with Barbara Overen Smith when she says that it is part of her nature—even after 40 years of lefse making—"to always try to improve the way I've done it." This is a master speaking. The beauty of mastering something—whether it's making lefse, playing music, or turning wood—is not that you will be called a master. No, the beauty is in the *practice* of maintaining an open mind, of not falling prey to arrogance and myopia. Mastery is in the patient questing and the experimenting that are fundamental to refinement and evolution.

I like that *The Last Word on Lefse* has not been the last word, that it needs refining and updating. Yes, I take satisfaction in how well the "How to Make Lefse" section has held up over 25 years. With photos, humor, stories, and poetry tucked in, the 12-step tutorial is still a very good reference for those wanting to learn to make lefse. But I like even more that there are tips in that section I no longer find useful. Thanks to what I've learned along the way, I have evolved and not stayed stuck in the Gospel According to Gary. Four examples of changes:

1. To lift a rolled-out lefse from pastry board to grill, I formerly advised: Lay a lefse stick on the edge of the round, and flip the edge over the stick with your finger. Then wrap the lefse around the stick by rotating the stick toward the center of the round. Pick up the stick, and unroll the round on the grill. Now, I know that's too much fussing. Just slide the stick under the lefse and lift the round over to the grill.

2. My fitted pastry-board cover was once the standard white. Now I use a cover that I dyed blue. Not only does this add color to the predominantly snowy lefse world, but the blue also makes it easier to detect sticky spots that can develop when rolling round after round. The potential trouble spot appears as a darker blue because it has less flour.

3. From time to time, I'm willing to use instant potatoes. I know, I know: It was heresy to suggest such a thing when I wrote *The Last Word on Lefse.* But I have tasted plenty of good instant-potato lefse from many lefse makers who still appear to have all their marbles. Using instant potatoes saves on time and labor, and sometimes I want to save on both. Plus, Jacobs Lefse

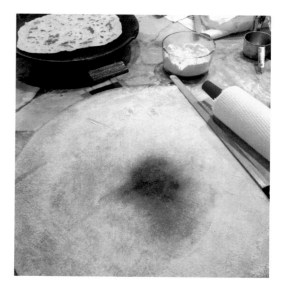

A blue pastry board cover helps a roller detect sticky spots. The potential trouble spot appears darker blue because it has less flour.

Bakeri in Osakis, Minnesota, has always used an instant-potato mix, and last December Jacobs won the WCCO Viewers' Choice for Best Lefse in Minnesota.

4. I no longer chill my dough overnight in a refrigerator before rolling.

What—No Chill!?!?

At one point in my lefse life, I outright dismissed the suggestion of not chilling my dough overnight or at least half a day. Not chill the dough? Nonsense! You *must* chill your dough. That's just the way it's done. It's traditional. It makes sense: Cool dough is less sticky and absorbs less flour, which is good because more flour equals tougher lefse. And to suggest otherwise was not evolutionary; it was revolutionary.

Well, my lefse friends, the Lefse Revolution is on!

This is a quiet revolution, of course. What else would it be with Scandinavians involved? It first came to my attention from two lefse luminaries: Eunice Stoen of Decorah, Iowa, and Elida Peterson of Rushford, Minnesota, both featured in *The Last Word on Lefse*. "They wouldn't think of refrigerating their potatoes," I wrote in the

David Hofstad gives away nearly 1,100 rounds of lefse yearly—and swears by rolling dough that is not chilled.

how-to section. "Eunice said it's not necessary. Just cool the potatoes to room temperature and go to the next step. And Elida said refrigerated potatoes 'sweat,' and anytime you have standing water around a batch of lefse you've got trouble. She let hers cool to room temperature, covering the bowl with a paper towel, so moisture can escape—so the dough can 'breathe,' as she put it."

I was enjoying so much success by chilling my dough overnight that I pooh-poohed these pioneers of the No Chill movement. No Chill was an anomaly, I thought, something peculiar to Eunice and Elida. I never imagined this practice would still be used—and even trumpeted—25 years later when I made my rounds with lefse makers for this book. But sure enough, Jean Olson of Deerwood, Minnesota, is a No Chiller—and she's a past champion of the Potato Days Festival's National Lefse Cook-off. She smugly smiles at non–No Chillers, thumbing her nose at what she calls "the Norwegian ladies in heaven looking down and saying, 'You can't do it that way! Those are warm potatoes!'"

And then there is David Hofstad of Cheverly, Maryland. If you were casting a movie and looking for a lefse revolutionary, David simply would not do. He's a friendly, 75-year-old tax-and-financial-planning guy, for goodness sakes. Not only is he a No Chiller, but he also doubles down and uses instant potatoes. Keep in mind, this is not a newbie who once a year dabbles with his dough. He's a lefse lifer.

In junior high in Madison, Minnesota, David started helping his mother, Alice Hofstad, who sold potato lefse. "Before I'd go to school, she had me turning," he said.

David went to college and took a job in the East. In the mid-1980s, he said, "Hey, I don't want to lose this tradition of making lefse around Christmastime." Alice came to visit and spent a couple of days teaching David the finer points of lefse making. He's been rolling ever since. Now he has a major production on his hands each November.

"I don't sell it like my mother did, but I give it away," said David. "I send to relatives and friends. I deliver it to neighbors and to my clients. This past year I baked 1,110 lefse. I mail lefse all over the country, and it's getting expensive with overnight mailing at $22.95 a package. I keep doing it because the recipients say, 'This is lefse like my grandmother used to make.' They love it, and it's a nice way to remember my mother."

As Christmas approaches, David does a batch of lefse at night after dinner and a batch during the day, about 60 rounds in 24 hours. "I end up watching a lot of TV," he said, laughing. "Lefse making is all about the old saying: It is more blessed to give than to receive. Lefse is part of Christmas. If you can give something at Christmas that people really like, that makes us all happier."

"All good," I said, "but why use instant potatoes?"

"I use Betty Crocker Potato Buds," David said. "I do that because my mother changed over from real potatoes; she just didn't have the time in her lefse business. She always said buds were better than flakes. I don't know why, but buds cut down on the time and preparation. I don't think buds affect the taste. If you look at the contents on the box, it's 99 percent potatoes."

"And what about rolling warm dough?" I protested. "That's lefse-making heresy!"

"Some bakers say that you allow the potato dough to cool down to room temperature [or cool in a refrigerator] before you begin to knead the flour into the dough," David said. "I have found I have *much* better luck in rolling out the dough if I add flour to the potato dough while it is still warm, almost hot."

Whoa. That's *righteous!*

Lefse in an Hour?

Amy Marquard, 45, of Foley, Minnesota, is not in the No Chill camp. But she is on the front lines of the Lefse Revolution because she uses techniques and products of her own creation to make lefse in an unheard-of amount of time: one hour—and that includes a chilling period.

I had to see this, so I made arrangements with Amy to meet at her home. On a warm August day blessed with a beautiful breeze, which fluttered Amy's kitchen curtains, I asked why she had created new products and methods and become a flag bearer in the Lefse Revolution.

"You know, everything we do is because that was how someone else taught us to do it—and we don't always think about why," Amy said. "We just do it because that was how someone else did it. And they did it that way because that's how someone else did it."

Amy didn't begin as a lefse revolutionary. She learned to make lefse after joining the Gustavus Adolphus Lutheran Church in Foley and pitching in to make lefse for the church's fall dinner. She taught her son, Gunnar, to roll lefse at 5 years old, and he caught on quickly to the art of rolling as well as eating lefse. He holds the Eats-the-Most-Lefse title in the house, she said.

When her children became teens, Amy joined the Lefse Revolution out of necessity. Her daughter, Audra, was raising funds for a high school senior class trip to Spain. While others sold candy bars, Audra raised $1,000 by selling lefse, which she and Amy made from 85 pounds of potatoes.

This dynamic duo realized early in their mass production that they needed to speed up their process. "Our cooling-towel setup was clumsy," said Amy. With each cooked lefse, they'd futz too much to cover the lefse without their cooling towels folding and bunching at the edges. She wanted a way to one-handedly uncover and cover the stack of rounds.

Amy Marquard has created techniques and products to make lefse in an hour.

Amy invented the Original Lefse Cuddler. This 15-by-29½-inch, double-thickness cotton dishtowel is about the size of a pillowcase. It has two seams sewn in the middle to facilitate folding in half to cover the cooked lefse. A knobbed red rod slides through a slot sewn at one end so that lefse bakers toting lefse on a stick in one hand can grab the rod with the other hand and open and close the Cuddler. You place unfolded lefse on the Cuddler, cover the round, and let it cool and become tender. You can place lefse from a 5-pound batch in the Cuddler for up to 4 hours, and then package the rounds in plastic and refrigerate or freeze them, said Amy.

Word spread about the Cuddler. The *St. Cloud Times* wanted to do a feature. The writer asked Amy to make lefse during the interview, and that request got Amy's creative juices flowing again. "I didn't want to make a big batch," Amy said, "but what if I scaled down the recipe from 5 pounds to 2 pounds of potatoes? Two potatoes weigh about 2 pounds, and I did some 7th-grade algebra to figure out how much butter, sugar, salt, and flour I needed for the small batch. So that's where the 'Two-Potato Frying-Pan Lefse in About an Hour' recipe came from."

Here's the recipe:

2	**potatoes**
1	**tablespoon butter**
¼	**teaspoon sugar**
⅛	**teaspoon salt**
¼	**cup flour**

"You make the dough but don't add the flour initially," said Amy. "The batch is so small that you can put it in the freezer for 20 to 30 minutes and get it down to the right temperature to be able to roll it. Of the hour it takes to do the recipe, half the time is just waiting for the dough to cool. It makes about 10 rounds, enough for dinner and a little more for breakfast. If you just want to eat lefse without the big production, it's a nice way to make it."

The Cuddler is one of Amy Marquard's labor-saving inventions for making lefse.

Amy demonstrated the process. First she peeled two potatoes, and each was 3½ inches long after peeling. Then she quartered the potatoes so each piece would cook at the same rate. She put the spuds in potted water on the stove, turned on the burner, and covered the pot. Boiling took 11½ minutes.

She riced the potatoes once (no mashing) and pressed them to the sides and bottom of a 5-by-9-inch glass baking dish. Next she added the butter, sugar, and salt. The butter melted on the warm potatoes and mixed with the sugar and salt; if the melting and mixing is incomplete, Amy said, pop the dish in the microwave. The goal was lefse dough spread thinly over the surface of the baking dish. She covered the dish with a paper towel and put it in her freezer.

Lefse Lite

After the dough had cooled sufficiently, Amy added the flour and was ready to roll. She used two other products that came about as the result of asking herself this question: "If I want to make a quick little batch of lefse in an hour, do I really want to drag out my big griddle and big rolling board?"

Her answer: no. So Amy created the Flour Filler, a rectangular piece of cotton-polyester cloth a little wider than the length of a rolling pin. She showed me how to use it. She rolled her sock-covered rolling pin back and forth over 3 tablespoons of flour spread on the Flour Filler. The pin picked up just enough flour to prevent sticking when rolling each round.

Amy also designed the Rotate-a-Round, a 10-inch or 16-inch cotton-polyester piece used to roll lefse and rotate the rolling surface in order to get a round lefse. It's a mini–pastry cloth that is great for rolling on the road. It worked beautifully for Amy as she efficiently rolled round after round.

The Flour Filler and the Rotate-a-Round are backed with rubber shelving material, which prevents the products from slipping around on the rolling surface. Another Amy-designed product, Tradition in a Tote, holds all your lefse-making gear, "everything but the frying pan," Amy said. Use it to store, grab, and go.

Speaking of frying pan, Amy's method does not require the conventional lefse grill. She uses a pancake griddle and an infrared thermometer to indicate when the griddle surface is 475 degrees. Amy said the thermometer is nice but not necessary. You can figure out when the griddle is hot enough by checking for rising bubbles in a baking round. If they don't form, the griddle is too cool.

By the way, Amy's Lefse in an Hour recipe yielded 14 nine-inch rounds in just a little over an hour.

Future Looks Good

As Amy cleaned up from lefse making and then prepped a lunch of fresh, delicious lefse, Gouda and Monterey jack cheese, salami and ham, homemade bread, and sliced tomatoes from her garden, we talked about her drive to come up with new products and methods.

"The Sons of Norway locally asked me to do a demonstration, and my contact person said, 'I've read your website [www.lefse land.com] and we're excited to have you come. But you should know there have been people in our group who have been making lefse longer than you have been alive.' I'm like, 'You invited me.' But I think she was just trying to give me fair warning."

But by and large, the reception to Amy's ways in Lefse Land has been good because people appreciate that she is just trying to bring potential lefse makers with time constraints into the fold.

"People may not make lefse because of the time involved or because they can buy it—or they just wait for someone else to make it," Amy said. "I teach lefse making, and I love the stories, the feedback after classes. They say 'Thank you so much for doing this. It made me remember how my grandma used to be in the basement or over the cookstove. Now I feel there's a chance I can do this on my own. I have so much confidence now. This is not hard. This is something I can do.'

"I just have so much anxiety about people wanting to learn how to do this. It can take so much time, but now with the Lefse in an Hour, I think it is more accessible to more people."

I thought about how much Amy was like me when I wrote *The Last Word on Lefse.* Her concern, like mine, is to preserve a threatened and cherished tradition. We both teach lefse-making classes. She makes lefse products, and I write lefse books. I was comforted that she represented the future and was leading a younger wave of lefse makers. And it was especially gladdening when this leader of the Lefse Revolution sent me off with a sweetly traditional thought: "Lefse making is such a strong part of our heritage, and lefse is an edible treasure."

The first time I tried making lefse with my girls, no, it did not go well. It was a nightmare. My girls called it Pretzel Donut Lefse Balls because the lefse ended up too thick. The potatoes were too moist and goopy, and I kept the dough out at room temperature too long. So it got sticky. We just kept adding flour to make them not so watery, and that was a big mess. The girls dipped them in butter and sugar and cinnamon, and they said it tasted good. But it wasn't lefse. So I did some research and asked ladies at church what I could do better. I improved a lot, and this year it turned out great. I froze some, and then when we traveled for Thanksgiving, I had a package in my suitcase. So 20 of us had lefse in Los Angeles for Thanksgiving.

—Kristin Klinefelter, 40, Grand Rapids, Minnesota

THE LEFSE LADIES IN MINNIE'S BASEMENT

Before the days of commercial lefse makers, Scandinavian stores like Ingebretsen's in Minneapolis relied on individual women, mostly, to meet the intense demand for lefse at the holidays. One such woman was Thelma Quale.

Thelma was the mother of James Quale, 72, of York, Maine, who grew up in a Norwegian family in Benson, Minnesota. He spoke only Norwegian until age 5. Lefse was a staple, recalled James, made once or twice a week along with bread.

"When I was about 10 years old, back around 1956, I moved to Minneapolis," James said. "And my mother had a good friend named Minnie Haugen. All the lefse that Minne made was delivered to Ingebretsen's store on 16th Avenue and Lake

Thelma Quale stands between Olga and Marvin Arneson, her sister-in-law and brother. Years ago, Thelma made lefse for Ingebretsen's Scandinavian store in Minneapolis.

Street. Minnie lived nearby on 31st Street and Bloomington Avenue South.

"At the holidays, Minnie gathered four or five friends in her basement to bake lefse for Ingebretsen's. My mother and I lived across the street from Minnie. There were also ladies in Minneapolis who took the bus to Minnie's house and slept there while they made lefse for Ingebretsen's. They'd

James Quale, who spoke only Norwegian until age 5, says lefse was a staple in his childhood home.

start early in the morning with boiling potatoes and ricing and mixing the dough, and all day long they'd roll lefse. Minnie's husband, Melvin, would bake on a double grill-top gas stove.

"It seems to me they got paid by the piece. There were two rollers, and others who would put lefse under dishcloths for cooling. Somebody else packaged them. Mimeographed papers listing the lefse ingredients were put inside the package, and the package was sealed with a hot plate. Packages went in a box, and Melvin would put the boxes in the car and make deliveries two to four times a day. Ingebretsen's would take as much as was made.

"It was hard, hard work, a seven-days-a-week operation. Everybody knew everybody, and everybody had a good time. These were all friends, and many had known each other since school.

"This lefse making would go on until the day before Thanksgiving, when everybody had to go home to prepare for the holiday. Then the day after Thanksgiving, they'd all come back and make lefse until the day before Christmas. It was quite a production. And I got recruited to turn the rounds in Minnie's basement after school. That was my early introduction to making lefse."

17
Lefse Tales, Lefse Tips

Getting the dough just right, I think,
is nine-tenths of the secret in making lefse.

–David Hofstad, 75, Cheverly, Maryland

Scandinavians, as saddled with stoicism as they are, do manage to tell a very good story—if you can get them to open up. Lefse gets them to open up.

When I ran my ¹⁄₁₂-page, four-color ad in *Viking* magazine asking lefse makers to email me their tales and tips, the response was excellent. Everybody, it seemed, had a lefse tale to share. I interviewed all responders either by phone or in person. This chapter features a dozen firsthand accounts and one interview, given anonymously because it dealt with confession of a crime.

A *WHEE* OF A TIME

"In October of 2000, we put word out that we're making lefse, so come on over and have some fun. My daughter-in-law and my aunt and her daughter came from Des Moines. My sister-in-law and her daughter and granddaughters came from Eau Claire. My niece came from Milwaukee, my aunt came from Sioux Falls, and my daughter-in-law came from Minneapolis. We made 50 pounds of potatoes into lefse. We had aprons made that said 'Lefse Fest 2000' and had our recipe on it. I gave everybody an apron when they got there.

"Now, the little kids are grown, and what the older people like is the connection of the cousins. They are all spread out and hardly know each other. So that's nice that they all look forward to it. We usually have good snacks and stuff, and then about 5 p.m. we open a bottle of wine and make a dinner. A lot of people spend the night, and then we have a nice breakfast the next day before everybody leaves. We just have a *whee* of a time.

"It's all about making the connections, you know? A lot of times when you're all spread out, you get together only for funerals. Well, *ick*, who wants to get together for just funerals? Get together for something fun! My aunt Marilyn Desey died three years ago, and she was a pistol. She was so funny every year we saw her for our Lefse Fest. She'd just love to come. She'd sit and drink beer and tell funny stories. We really miss her. And you know, nobody's going to be around forever."

–Karen Mattson, 69, Austin, Minnesota

TIP: "This is a tip on making round rounds from Charlotte Jacobson and Pearl Elbekrog, who made lefse in the Sons of Norway lodge in Stoughton for 50 years. In fact, I had to wash a lot of pots and pans for a long time before I worked my way up and got to actually making lefse. You take your round ball of lefse and with your thumb make a little cup in the center. That way the center doesn't stay too thick. You want the round to have even thickness. And then when you start rolling, you roll from the middle out to make it a round. The other trick, honestly, is to use little, tiny rollers to roll. They make a nice round lefse. The edges don't get out of hand, and if they do you just cut them off with a knife. You can always round it off that way if you need to."

—Susan Slinde, 77, Stoughton, Wisconsin

TIP: "I used to take my metal spatula and cut the edges of the lefse to make a round round. But then after buying from some of these places, I saw that theirs were not round, not perfect. So the heck with it. I don't worry about it now."

—Mavis Cook, 84, Spooner, Wisconsin

VIKINGS, PACKERS, LEFSE

"A friend and I were saving our money for a trip out to Canton, Ohio, to see Brett Favre [of the Green Bay Packers] inducted into the NFL Hall of Fame. He retired, and so we got tickets—and then he went to play for someone else [the Minnesota Vikings]. We decided we weren't interested and got our deposit back. Then I wondered, 'What can I do with this?' So I went off and bought all the lefse tools and a griddle and your book [*The Last Word on Lefse*], and I jumped into it. We get a bottle of wine and make a day of it, and it works out pretty well.

"Three Christmases ago, I was told that I had to open the first present. We usually don't do something like this, but I said OK. A lot of cameras were at the ready, and when I opened the present, it was my grandmother Myrtle's lefse rolling pin. She used to wrap her pin in tinfoil, not a sock, to prevent the flour from getting in the grooves. My dad said that I might as well have it, and so I have two pins now. That was very neat."

—Dave Glomstad, 53, La Crescent, Minnesota

TIP: "The lefse toolbox was my wife's [Becky Glomstad's] inspiration. She said, 'You're going to make lefse about twice a year, and you'll have all your equipment rattling around in the drawers and won't be able to find anything when you need it.' So I came up with a box with a sliding top, and everything related to lefse fits in there nicely. I had a local rosemaler, Sharon Henke, paint on the cover. The toolbox holds the lefse pin, two sticks, my recipe, and my rolling pad cover."

—Dave Glomstad, 53, La Crescent, Minnesota

Dave Glomstad's
lefse toolbox–brilliant!

TIP: "I have a special board so that I'm rolling without bending over. It's about 8 inches thick, and I put it on the countertop. It's about 30 inches long and 20 inches wide and made of compressed wood. It's heavy. It makes a big difference so I don't have to bend over."

—Lyle Nelson, 75, Mesa, Arizona

FLATTERED OR GOLDARNED MAD

"I was a nosy little kid and always had my hands in there with my mother, Annie Andreson Anderson, when she made lefse. I remember the bread wrappers were kind of waxy, and she would clean off the top of the cookstove with the wrapper before and after making lefse.

"First time my husband, Tom, and I made lefse, we got the equipment, and so what does he do? He called his parents to come and watch us. She was a good ol' Norwegian cook and knew a lot about making lefse. What could I do? I had to go ahead and make it. I didn't have a lefse stick and told Tom that I gotta have a stick. So he took a stick out of a window shade and carved it off on the end so it was pointed. And the lefse turned out pretty good; they liked it. Did they offer advice? They didn't dare. The next time we were going to make it, he invited his aunt and uncle to come and watch. I thought that I either should be flattered or goldarned mad.

"My husband turned the lefse for me, and he was so good at it. Except after the first one or two that came off the grill, he'd be gone over the cupboard to put butter and cinnamon and sugar on it. I'd say, 'Get back here! You gotta turn that!'

"I was quite the star lefse maker. I'm kind of a dim star now. Last year, I didn't make lefse at all. The kitchen where I'm at now is not very handy for making it. I'm hoping I can go over to my daughter's and make lefse. I get very tired, but otherwise, I'm all for it. I hope I make lefse again, because I like mine best."

—Mavis Cook, 84, Spooner, Wisconsin

TIP: "Every event that involves family involves food, because food is love."

—Marcella Richman, 82, cookbook author,
Valley City, North Dakota

MARY'S LEFSE LEGACY

"My grandma Ella Bjorgaard taught me that you hang your grilled rounds over the back of the chair on a towel and then put another towel on top. Then you quick take the top towel off, put another hot lefse on the chair back, and then cover with the towel again. That way, they stay soft and don't get hard.

"Don't think you can do a lot of other things on lefse day. Plan it so that all you have to do is lefse. Because the only time I run into problems is if I try to run around and do a bunch of other things at the same time.

"Each year when I make lefse, my first couple rounds sort of look like amoebas. And we laugh and say, 'These we're eating right away. No one is going to see them!'

"Lefse making was lots of hours of kitchen time with the kids and without distractions. As they got older, I treasured that more and more. When you have high school kids, it's pretty rare that they'll stand in the kitchen and talk with you for hours. We usually listened to *The Nutcracker* when we rolled. Now I have grandchildren, and they come from Madison on lefse-making day. My kids really like that and want that experience for their kids. And they all seem to like eating the lefse, too.

"I really do like tying all the generations together with something traditional like lefse making. It's worth all the work to do it. I like being able to pass this on. My son, Seth Pearson, will probably be the one who continues with lefse. I like thinking that someday he'll be making it with his kids and grandkids, and he'll tell them about making it with me.

"I have to admit that about five years ago I switched to instant potatoes. I know, it's sort of a sacrilege. I'm glad my grandma doesn't know. I shouldn't even have told you that, but it's so much easier to handle!"

–Mary Bjorgaard, 65, Danbury, Wisconsin

———————

TIP: "One tip Grandma gave me a long time ago was to put just a bit of sugar in the recipe, and the rounds brown nicer."

–Mary Bjorgaard

GOOD THINGS TAKE TIME

"My father, Kenneth Lysne, passed away ... and my mother, Iva Lysne, was unusually sad after the funeral. My friend said, 'Is there something we should do, Iva?' She said, 'The thing I am most sad about is I don't have anyone to make lefse with anymore.' That fall, the friend, my husband, Walter, and I went to Mom's house to make lefse. And we had a grand time. She taught us things she had learned over the years from her mother and grandmother.

"I learned to make lefse at age 50. From talking with fellow baby boomers in the store [The Nordic Shop], that's quite true. Customers come in and say, 'I need to learn how to do this, to buy the proper equipment and make lefse.' It was typical of the parents of baby boomers to take it upon themselves to do these things without asking for much help. And now we need to learn how to do this because our parents aren't able or aren't alive.

"I feel strongly that lefse making will continue. There are enough people who want to learn to make it efficiently and properly, and the fun part is children want to learn. When we had our family gathering of 30 people this fall, several genera-tions were rolling lefse. We even had little girls 5 or 6 years old rolling, and some of them were quite good.

"People are fascinated by lefse making. We'll have people from other cultures come by when we're making lefse, and they'll talk about some of the foods in their culture. As we share ideas and sample recipes, it's important to learn from other people about their heritage.

"Regarding lefse making, good things take time. ... That's pretty Scandinavian."

–Louise Hanson, 66, Rochester, Minnesota

—————

TIP: "I like to put a little flour under the pastry board so that the board spins easily when I roll lefse. That helps rotate the board and keep the round a little more even as far as thickness goes."

–Connie Rasmusson, 54, Story City, Iowa

TIP: "I fold each lefse and put waxed paper or parchment paper between each folded lefse. Then I cover with a towel. That softens the edges."

–Mary Lou Peterson, 71, Minnetonka, Minnesota

Mary Lou Peterson makes lefse in her kitchen.

48 A DAY

"I start baking lefse the last week in July and bake every day until November. I have to have 750 lefse ready by the first Saturday in November, when there is a big lutefisk dinner here. I also sell 300 packages of lefse at this dinner, with three lefse per package. I sell them for $6 per package. All I can do is 48 a day. I tire out because it takes about three hours. To do more, I'd have to have more space for cooling and stuff. I sell through bake sales, and then a lot of people know about me so I sell out of the house, too, through December. I get up every day and I make lefse. And every night around 11 o'clock, I make dough and put it in the fridge so it's ready for the following morning. It gives me something to do. People have my number and will call to ask for lefse."

–Lyle Nelson, 75, Mesa, Arizona

THINKING OF MOM

"I used to tell my kids about lefse because my mother used to make it. They said, 'Well, Dad, you helped Grandma. Why can't you just make it here?' So I bought my equipment and started making it. The biggest problem I had in the beginning was figuring out how much pressure to put on the rolling pin. Once I got that, I was fine.

"I have sons in Oregon and California, and we all get together in Vegas, where my oldest son lives. And they and the grandkids all want to make lefse. I just stand back and advise. It's a big family thing at least once a year.

"When I'm making lefse, my mother [Francis Hurst] comes to mind. Definitely. As I roll, I can still see her standing there making lefse in her kitchen. Every time I make it, I think of her."

–Larry Hurst, 75, Grand Junction, Colorado

Larry Hurst herds his kids and grandkids to Las Vegas for a yearly lefse fest.

TIP: "I remember once when we used red potatoes. Can't use red potatoes. The dough turned into ... what was the movie, *The Blob That Devoured New York*? Something like that. It was just a big, gooey, sticky, messy blob. You could have built a brick wall and used the dough as mortar."

–Dan Olson, 66, Golden, Colorado

OH, WHAT DOES *SHE* KNOW?

"There are different old ladies, uh, different people that come every year to help out making lefse at [Mondovi Methodist] church, and while the grandmas are making dough and running around and putting stuff on carts and writing down the schedule, I'm usually teaching.

"Grandma [Lisa Bishopp] will say to the new ones, 'If you just go over to that station, that young girl will teach you and help you do it.' Their reaction is, like, 'Wait, are you sure?' It's super funny how they react. They are really superstitious, like 'Does she really know what she's doing?' One of them said, 'You do know how to make lefse, right?' And I said I've been making it since I've been 3. The rolling part is the hardest and the part they really mess up."

—Alana Bishopp, 11, Eau Claire and Eleva, Wisconsin

Alana Bishopp, 11, has been making lefse since she was 3. Great-grandma Linda Johnston is behind Alana.

TIP: "I think it's necessary to have a discussion on lefse sticks. Our family members are skinny-stick people, and I have a girl-friend who is a fat-stick person. I like the skinny stick for lifting lefse from the floured board to the grill. Why? Just because."

—Sally Norheim Dwyer, 62, Petersburg, Alaska

Hardanger or Hard Lefse

Unlike potato lefse, Hardanger or hard lefse isn't made with potatoes—just Crisco or lard dissolved in milk, with sugar, salt, and flour added later. It is rolled and grilled like potato lefse, then stacked and stored in a cool, dry place. No refrigeration needed. In this dry state, hard lefse is crisp, unlike soft potato lefse, and is edible for months. Unrefrigerated potato lefse must be eaten in a few days after grilling. When you want to eat hard lefse, dip it in water, let the excess drip off, and place it between towels or waxed paper until soft and rollable.

MAKING LEFSE IS SHARING LOVE

"About a dozen women of the Sons of Norway lodge met to make Hardanger lefse for the Astoria Scandinavian Midsummer Festival in June, which began 50 years ago in Astoria, Oregon. The story goes that they were pretty traditional. You didn't do much talking or laughing back then, and they weren't very good at telling you what to do. You were supposed to *know* what to do. Of course, they weren't happy if you didn't do it right. About 25 years ago, I started going over and helping. About 15 years ago, as those women got older, I became more involved with leading the charge. About 2007 or 2008, they finally trusted me enough to allow me to take over.

"Many women who are helpers also have husbands who come and help, and I asked our group what the founding women, who started lefse making for the festival all those years ago, would have said about letting the men help us. The response was the founding women would have said, 'It's about time!'

"My favorite part about working the Scandinavian festival is the people coming to buy lefse. They remember this kind of lefse, Hardanger lefse, and it's fun to watch them take a bite and remember all those food memories that come flowing back. That makes it worth it, and so I feel pretty dedicated to continuing the tradition.

"With the different times of your life, you have different levels of busyness. The interest in lefse making is there, and I usually get a few recruits every year at our festival. Some people may only come three or four hours, but that's getting them started and they enjoy it. And we get non-Norwegian people learning to make lefse, which is pretty fun.

"Lefse-making is the sharing of love."

–Lou Ann Thorsness, 60, Salem, Oregon

TIP: "I decided I had to have a reproducible recipe. By reproducible, I mean standardizing the moisture content of the dough. That's why I commit the worst of lefse sins by using instant potatoes. I also weigh in grams versus ounces. You don't have fractions when you weigh in grams. If you weigh in ounces, you'll have fractions, which are harder to deal with. I think in metrics, so grams are not a problem for me."

–Roger Westland, 88, Fountain Hills, Arizona

SOAK LEFSE? NO

"I remember Mom, Evelyn Erickson Hill, making lefse on a cookstove, which had to be a challenge with controlling the heat because she'd use wood or coal or corn cobs or whatever we had for fuel. They learned the skill of controlling that heat.

"I'm talking about the flour kind of lefse that gets brittle and hard and that you can store for months and months. And then you soak it between towels when you get ready to eat it. But I have to watch how I word that because I had a friend of my sister who didn't know anything about hard lefse. They told her that you just soak it, and so she just put it in a sink full of water and let it sit there. It totally disintegrated, of course. No, you run it under water and put it between towels.

"The first time I ate potato lefse, I thought the makers just didn't know how to make the right kind of lefse. We once went to Nordic Fest in Decorah, Iowa, and went all over that town looking for flour lefse. They looked at us like, 'What do you mean?' They didn't know about our kind, and we learned about potato lefse.

"Once the kids grow up and leave the state, I want them to have a little bit of heritage. I feel at least with lefse they'll have the food. Also, as the kids get older, with technology and social media and things like that, lefse making is one of the few things we do together and look forward to doing. What could be more important than that? It's like, 'Leave your cell phone in the car, put on some Christmas music, roll out the lefse, and have fun eating the first piece.' That's what I love about this as a grandmother, when the little ones ask, 'Nana, when are we going to make lefse?' That makes my heart sing.

"You have to keep trying. It's not like those first lefse rounds out are going to be perfect and wonderful. They're going to be mis-shapen like Africa or Aus-tralia, too thick or too thin, burned. But don't give up. Keep trying. That attitude applies to a lot of things in life. You may not be success-ful the first time. It takes patience and practice. If you stick with it, it pays off."

—Carolyn Yorgensen, 67, Ames, Iowa

Carolyn Yorgensen: "Once the kids grow up and leave the state, I want them to have a little bit of heritage. I feel at least with lefse they'll have the food."

TIP: "If your lefse rounds have a few crinkly edges, either now or after you defrost them, you can recapture their soft freshness by putting them in the microwave for seven seconds or so."

—David Hofstad, 75, Cheverly, Maryland

HARD LEFSE MADE THE PASSAGE EASIER

"Grandma Johanna Grimsley Tieg told stories about her and her sister coming from Norway on a boat. She came from central Norway, but there were people from all parts of the country. Well, some had made yeast bread or potato lefse, and after a week or so it started to mold. But Grandma had made hard lefse, and there was always fresh water on the boat so they could soak and regenerate it. So they always had this food to eat because they always had hard lefse. I was so intrigued with that story, that hard lefse was part of their survival when they came from Norway.

"Until I was 25, making lefse was always something my dad, Mervin Tieg, did. He always used to make all of it at holidays. But at that point I said, 'I want to see what you're doing here. I want to know how you're doing things so when somebody needs to step in, I can be the one.'

"Quite honestly, I had the undivided attention of my kids when we made lefse. We laughed, and we had more good conversations just making lefse.

"I make quite a bit of lefse at the holidays. It's great because I'm able to make a special tradition happen for a lot of people. It's just kind of a joyous, magical time."

—Connie Rasmusson, 54, Story City, Iowa

TIP: "Place the rolling pin in the middle of the lefse dough ball and roll to the edge—but lift the pin before you hit the edge. It makes the edges too thin if you don't."

—Bill Wilson, 69, Scotts Mills, Oregon

Bill Wilson teaches the finer points of lefse making to his granddaughters, Heidi, left, and Hailey Gerdts.

TIP: "I start with a little round patty and lightly flour both sides. I always use a pastry board with the cover that has red rings. When I can see the rings through my rolled-out lefse, I know it's thin enough."

–Shirley Evenstad, 71, Minneapolis, Minnesota

Shirley Evenstad rolls her lefse thin, and she created the rosemaling that appears in this book.

THE POWER OF LEFSE

When Cordell Keith Haugen was growing up on a farm in Kittson County in northern Minnesota, he remembered lefse as a staple made almost daily on a wood-burning stove. "We were poor, but we ate well," he said. The following is an excerpt from Haugen's previously published story about lefse and his "stern and commanding" grandmother Mari Haugen. The story, used here with Haugen's permission, is a testament to the power of lefse—how it can even make a stoic Scandinavian smile.

"It was in the early 1940s, during World War II, and visits to my paternal grandmother were major outings. Gasoline and other rationed items were in such short supply that no one went far, or often. Grandma lived on a small farm about seven miles from the little town where we had lived since my father lost our farm during the Great Depression, before I was born. Grandpa had died in 1903 when my father was only 8 years old, and Grandma was really a link with the past. Her English was limited to a few phrases, only those most necessary to the hard life to which she had become accustomed.

Cordell Keith Haugen says he knew his grandma's smile meant one thing: lefse.

"The one I remember most was, 'You want lefse?' Yes, she had that singsong brogue, which people make fun of today when they joke about Minnesota Norwegians. But to us it was like the voice of an angel. When she asked that question, she was singing our song. My brother Jim and I were the youngest in the family, and we were always less frightened of Grandma, with her stern countenance, when she made such an offer. We would nod our reply and wait for a sign. She would almost smile and then point to the bedroom, which opened off of the living room. It was our cue.

"We'd run the few steps to her bedroom, lift the spread, and from under the old frame bed we would slide out a huge box that kept the treasure. It was cold in there, far from the only stove in the home, and clearly the best place to store the staple. She didn't have an icebox. We would open the box and there, between sheets of wax paper, were dozens of huge lefse, folded once into half-rounds, each about 20 to 22 inches across.

"From her seat next to the old woodstove, on top of which she baked these gems, came Grandma's voice again. 'One,' she said firmly. 'One,' she would repeat in a voice as stern and commanding as her facial expression.

"We would each take one, cover the top layer again with the wax paper, and fold closed the dishtowel made from a flour sack. We'd close the box and timidly find our way back to the kitchen, where our mother had butter and sugar ready to finish up our treat.

"If we ate the whole thing, Grandma would wait for what seemed like forever and then ask, 'You want lefse?' And we'd repeat the exercise. Usually, two was all we could eat—two each, that is. But, if we were really hungry and she thought we could handle a third, the exercise was repeated. By then, you could see a smile of pleasure on her face.

"She knew the way to our hearts. She never hugged us, never kissed us, never told us that she loved us. But we knew. If she didn't love us, why would she have treated us to her lefse?"

–Cordell Keith Haugen, 76, Nuuanu Valley, Hawaii

TIP: "Almost always the potatoes are cooked with the skins on. Some like to peel first, but potatoes can lose the flavor of skin, and the skin makes the lefse have a more potato taste."

–Barbara Overen Smith, 76, Bend, Oregon

A BIG IRISHMAN NAMED ALAN DWYER

"My grandmother Tora Tviberg Norheim was from a town about an hour outside of Oslo. Her father was a farmer, and she made hard lefse. She always said, 'We don't do potato lefse. We're not peasants!'

"I would sit in a chair and watch my grandmother. She was a very strong woman and could roll out lefse like nobody's business. She'd flop it on top of the oil stove, which she had scrubbed and put flour on, and it was a beautiful thing to watch. It made me so proud that she was so strong and she could just nail that little, tiny egg-size ball into a 16- to 18-inch lefse. She was an excellent teacher and would sing little songs and tell us stories about her town in Norway while she did her lefse rolling. She always handed each kid two lefse, 'one for each hand, to keep you

Sally and Alan Dwyer enjoy a holiday outing in Alaska.

busy,' she'd say. My sister, Susan Norheim Flint, and I are like her. We're both big, strong women, and we make lefse and are passing it down to our nieces and grandchildren. In our town we are among the few left who make Hardanger lefse.

"When I made lefse for the first time by myself, it was kind of scary. I had in my mind my grandmother's mentoring on my shoulder. I was living in Juneau [Alaska], and I got on the phone with my sister, who was living in Los Angeles and is a little older and had made it. She kind of walked me through it. It was fine. It turned out perfect.

"One year the sophomore class wanted to raise money to go to Washington, D.C., for Close Up, and they borrowed a bunch of lefse grills, including mine and my sister's. They went to a hotel restaurant and made 1,500 sheets of potato lefse. They cooled them and put them in bags of four for freezing, and then they sold them for $10 a bag. In two days they made $15,000 to put toward their travel.

"The last time we made lefse, it was a double batch [70 sheets] for my husband's funeral. We weren't going to use store-bought lefse for my husband—no way. So there were four generations making the lefse that day. My husband would have been so happy with the little ones helping out. He was a roller, a big Irishman named Alan Dwyer."

–Sally Norheim Dwyer, 62, Petersburg, Alaska

LEFSE DRIVES PREACHER TO LARCENY

In the course of researching this book, I stumbled upon a nest of lefse larcenists. This case involved an honorable Norwegian family, so it was a delicate matter for discussion—and possibly for legal action.

The whistleblower for this lefse larceny chose to remain anonymous in exchange for full immunity and shelter in the witness-protection plan. She had agreed to name names but demanded her identity remain unspecified. Hence, the intriguing and decidedly non-Norwegian *nom de plume* used by this 35-year-old snitch from Minneapolis: Kirsten Desjardins (*desjardins* is French for "she who throws family under the bus").

Full disclosure: Accuracy with names and events revealed in this interview may have been a bit off because our tattletale's speech was consistently compromised by her tongue being firmly planted in her cheek.

Legwold: I know this is difficult to come forth with this crime, but please tell us about your family's lefse larceny.
Kirsten: It began because it was a matter of supply and demand. There was a finite amount of lefse made and therefore not enough to have as much as you wanted. This often led to a lot of pressure to keep your lefse after you had it buttered and sugared. Thus, there was stealing of lefse at the table.

Legwold: That's a heavy charge—stealing—to level at your own family, Kirsten. Are you sure about this?
Kirsten: Absolutely. You would put a lot of time into preparing your lefse, and then you'd set it on your plate to dish up mashed potatoes or turkey or corn. And then you'd turn back to your plate—only to see that the lefse was gone! (Tears.)

Legwold: Please, give yourself a minute (offering tissue). Now, did this larceny involve everyone in the family, or were there specific agitators?
Kirsten: Grandpa was very good at stealing lefse.

Legwold: Did Grandpa have a name?
Kirsten: Alfred Sevig, a Lutheran minister. ... He was very good

Mari Elise Sevig, left, and Kirsten Desjardins make lefse. Kirsten once blew the whistle on a nest of lefse larcenists.

at stealing lefse but also afraid that someone was going to steal his. One Thanksgiving he ate with just one hand—his other hand gripping with white knuckles his rolled-up lefse. At one point he even put the lefse in his inside suit coat pocket to keep it near his chest so nobody could steal it. Laundering was not on his mind; he was caught up in the moment of saving his lefse. Once he put time into buttering and sugaring lefse, he wanted to make sure *he* was the consumer, not someone else.

Legwold: *So, in the reverend's defense, could you say that he was lefse-impaired?*
Kirsten: Absolutely, lefse impaired his judgment. It was all he could focus on. Conversations and other things were going on, but at the forefront of his mind was lefse and making sure no one stole it.

Legwold: *Was the good reverend the sole instigator, or were there others?*
Kirsten: Mike Sevig, my father, may be guilty of starting it, as well as Uncle Paul Sevig. Both are good at stealing lefse.

Legwold: *What was—and still is, apparently—their modus operandi?*
Kirsten: Distraction. It was definitely up-close magic, getting us to look somewhere else for a moment and then employing a very quick sleight-of-hand so that it was barely noticeable—until later when you remembered that you had buttered and sugared your lefse and it was no longer there on your ... (Tears.)

Legwold: *Yes, I know this is difficult, Kirsten. You are doing very well. Just a few more questions. Did these vipers prey upon the young and infirm?*
Kirsten: No one was immune. It didn't matter how old you were; you had to be aware of where your lefse was at all times because you could certainly lose it.

Legwold: *How did you protect yourself when you were young?*
Kirsten: As a kid, I did just straight sugar on my lefse. No butter as a binder. I just rolled it tight enough so the sugar didn't drain out. Fewer people stole my lefse because it was less desirable.

Legwold: *Brilliant! Plus, you removed a step in the preparation and therefore could eat it faster.*
Kirsten: (Blushing and smiling) It was a quicker process from beginning to end, thank you, and it was slightly less desirable because I did it my way.

Legwold: *Has the lefse larceny changed since the passing of Grandpa?*
Kirsten: It has continued, but there is more lefse on hand and less urgency to steal. We make enough so there isn't a huge demand and a low supply. But I won't lie, there is still enjoyment in stealing someone's lefse after he or she has buttered and sugared it. It is quite satisfying to have someone else butter and sugar *your* lefse and to take advantage of that.

Legwold: *I must say, Kirsten, it sounds like you have become a lefse larcenist.*

Kirsten: (With brightness in her eyes) Well, you do develop a taste for stealing. You make sure someone is engaged in conversation ... someone beside you, the nearer the better. And then, with no small amount of adroitness, you *steal* his or her lefse.

Legwold: *Do you pick your prey, someone easily distractible, as you prepare a seating arrangement?*

Kirsten: I never really considered the seating arrangement strategically ... but now that you have mentioned it, prepping the meal and making the seating arrangement will be at the front of my mind going into a holiday gathering.

Legwold: *You mentioned that your family is now making more lefse, thus making it less of a controlled substance, if you will. How would you describe the lefse-making gatherings in your family?*

Kirsten: Lefse making in my family is a rather tense occasion. There is a lot of scrutiny based on who is doing something correctly and whether someone is flipping a round too soon or not soon enough. There are roles that need to be switched in order to appease people who feel that they could be doing something better. Lefse making is not a stress-free activity with the family, but rather you enter into it with the understanding that everything you do will be scrutinized.

Legwold: *Scrutinized?*

Kirsten: It really is sort of a perfectionistic activity where everyone has the best of intentions because all they want is the very best lefse. But the scrutiny is very difficult. There's a lot of pressure to not mess it up when someone else has put in the time to make the lefse dough. When you are the one rolling it out, when you are the one flipping it, there is a lot of pressure. A lot of time has been put into it, and you do not want to be the one ruining it.

Legwold: *What do you do to handle the pressure? Stress-reducing breathing exercises? Yoga? Counseling?*

Kirsten: I definitely could've benefited from a pre-lefse-making meditation, something that could've made me mindful. That definitely could've helped. Moving forward, the next time we get together to make a lefse, I probably will be more prepared emotionally and psychologically and in general for the pressure involved.

Legwold: *Two more questions, Kirsten. First, do you think there is a link between this pressure in making lefse with your family and the lefse larceny at family gatherings?*
Kirsten: There is definitely a relationship between the kind of family that has so much tension built up around having the perfect lefse and the family that would also steal said lefse. This would be an interesting case study. A lot could be learned about a family based on how they make lefse and whether or not they steal lefse.

Legwold: *Finally, what is your best tip for making lefse?*
Kirsten: When making lefse with my family and the rounds fall short of perfection, I find myself in a position of reminding everyone that we all care equally for the lefse and are trying the best we can. My focus is on staying calm, breathing deeply, and taking a break when I need to—just so I can handle the pressure. You want to be present in the process. When the family has too many cooks in the kitchen, it can be stressful. I want to remember that this is a joyful thing that brings families together. So to answer your question, my **TIP: Keep it light and stay calm.**

18
Lefse Fests

Lefse making is about as family-oriented as it gets. It's what we do at Christmastime. It's what we do when we all get together. It's memories. We usually make a batch of glogg and have that heating on the stove. Grandpa (me) lays out all the lefse equipment and starts rolling, and then the daughters come along and their husbands and children, who all take a shot at it. We've got Christmas carols playing in the background, and everybody is eating lefse hot off the grill. It doesn't get a whole lot better than that.

—Bill Wilson, 69, Scotts Mills, Oregon

When I pulled up to Gloria's house around 11 a.m., I kinda figured her family was going all out in their celebration of family, tradition, and lefse. I was greeted by a painted plywood figure of a woman merrily making lefse. She was planted upright in the front lawn, welcoming all those who ventured past her and also warning them to check their grumpiness at the door.

Inside, Gloria Fetty, 79, was hosting the annual family lefse fest in her narrow galley kitchen in Viroqua, Wisconsin (pop. 4,369 in 2014). All but one of Gloria's Gang were there, and the fest was in full swing. Crammed into the kitchen were her daughters Vicki Wilson, Sarah Spah, and Carla Cebula. "My other daughter, Ellen Berg, could not make it today, but she has always been here," Gloria told me. Other Gang members were sister-in-law Signe Peterson, son-in-law Randy Spah, granddaughter Jessie Reed, great-granddaughter Finley Reed, and Riley the dog.

The Gang had started the fest at 7:30 a.m. with peeling, boiling, and cooling 50 pounds of potatoes. Now they were rolling and lefse loose. The scene was indeed a celebration, laced with elements of a madcap M*A*S*H episode. Lefse doctors at five rolling stations fed four grills, which were humming and puffing steam heavenward from the rounds. Randy, in the role of Radar O'Reilly, was relegated to being the runner who carried dough balls from the cool garage to the hot kitchen. Randy tossed the dough balls rapid fire to rollers in need. The women rolled, gabbed, waved lefse sticks, gabbed, lanced bubbles rising from the grilling rounds (they said they didn't really know why),

A madcap lefse fest features Gloria's Gang, left to right: Randy Spah, Signe Peterson, Carla Cebula, Finley Reed, Jessie Reed, Vicki Wilson, Sarah Spah, and Gloria Fetty.

gabbed, turned lefse on the grill, and even danced as the spirit moved them.

Lefse Casualty

"Lefse down! Lefse down!"

Someone had rolled a round so thin that it tore during transport from rolling surface to grill. Whoops of laugher followed, but no one missed a beat as the lefse-making machinery was humming in high gear.

Lulls came when the women had to catch their breath and reload, but typically there were up to four conversations going on at once. Trying to keep track of the chatter was like following a laser-tag game, and it was tricky figuring out

After granddaughter Jessie floured up her hands and grabbed Gloria's buttocks, Gloria guffawed and said, "I don't know how I raised them, but I didn't do a good job!"

who said what. I called out a general compliment on the uniform white aprons with the owner's name sewn in red. Someone shouted that when the aprons were made, the seamstress joked: "Yeah, you're all Norwegian. You have to have your names on your aprons or you wouldn't know who you are."

As the Gang rolled on, the grilled lefse rounds were stacked on white dishtowel slings. Two "orderlies" transported full slings to a recovery room. They stacked the slings and covered them with a white sheet, allowing the lefse to rest, cool, and soften. The rounds would be divvied up later.

At one point, Jessie, clearly under the influence of lefse, floured up her hands and grabbed Gloria's buttocks, leaving white handprints on Gloria's blue jeans. Gloria guffawed and said, "I don't know how I raised them, but I didn't do a good job!"

To make up for such transgressions, which poor Gloria endured throughout the lefse fest, the Gang every so often broke out in a chorus of "G-L-O-R-I—Gloria!" Van Morrison wrote and popularized "Gloria" in 1964, but he'd play second fiddle to Gloria's Gang.

Lunch blessedly interrupted the "lefsepalooza." I was told a wine break (mercy me!) would highlight the late afternoon. I would be outta there, but I chuckled at the imagined scene. I asked Gloria how long she would keep doing the lefse fests.

"I don't know," she said, sighing with satisfaction. "Until I can't roll anymore, I guess. I have arthritis in my hands, but lefse making keeps me feisty. You gotta keep doing the things you've always done."

Vicki was putting soup and homemade bread on the dinner table. She would not hear of ever ending these fests. "Lefse kinda defines us as Norwegians," she said. "The Irish and Italians and others have their cultures, so this helps define us. We can talk about it to our friends, and it helps us know where we came from."

Following the fest, Vicki sent me an email saying, "We ended up packaging 210 lefse. Everyone was asleep on the couch by 7:30 p.m."

Frankly, I don't know how they lasted that long. I was pooped in the early afternoon when I staggered away from Gloria's lefsepalooza. My ears were ringing and my head was spinning with all the giddy, gabby, and grabby hubbub that had happened in Gloria's happenin' kitchen.

Lefse Fest 2.0

I first learned of the Hart Lefsefest on a visit to the Minnesota History Center. I had made my way to the information desk at the Gale Family Library. I asked a volunteer where I might find historical tidbits on lefse.

"Yes, you've come to the right place," said the volunteer, Roxanne Hart, 62, of St. Paul, Minnesota. "Um, are you Gary Legwold?"

Every author dreams of fame and fortune, but until then I had not experienced either. This was about as close as I would get to fame, so I was going to appreciate it. I blushed, smiled, and said I was.

Roxanne said she had enjoyed *The Last Word on Lefse* and had shared it with other members of the Hart Lefsefest. I asked about her fest, and she laughed. The family had been doing lefse

From left, Roxanne Hart, Nett Hart, and Craig Hart revived the Hart Lefsefest only after their family committed to less production and more fun.

fests for years but then stopped because no one was having any fun. It seemed the only way the family could bring back lefse fests was to shed some of its results-oriented Germanic ways.

I couldn't wait to hear the full story, so she said it was fine that I interview her and other family members at the next gathering.

The Hart Lefsefest was on a snowy Sunday in mid-December. Sixteen people attended, and most were clustered in the cozy kitchen around two rolling stations and one lefse grill. The table in the dining room was weighed down with a pot of homemade soup and all manner of appetizers, snacks, and desserts.

"This started in the late 1950s when we were children," said Roxanne. "My mother, Ann Hart, had a brother, John Augustin, who married a Norwegian woman, Janice. So the nod to welcome her into the family was the annual making of lefse. Four families with 28 grandchildren converged before Thanksgiving on the tiny house in Austin, Minnesota, owned by my grandparents Fred and Nora Augustin. They made enough lefse for the families for Thanksgiving and Christmas. Keep in mind this was about production; that was the overarching thing, that we were there to *make* lefse."

Men rolled and grilled in the basement. Women cooked potatoes upstairs and made dough balls. Kids were dough-ball runners who could graduate to towel assistants. "You started on towels," said Craig Hart, Roxanne's brother. "The uncles doing the grilling would call out 'Towel!' The kid assisting raised his towel and then lowered it once the round was placed for cooling. It was an honor to earn that position."

"How did you earn that honor?" I asked.

"I can't remember," said Craig, smirking. "I was honored at such an early age."

Towelers became lefse flippers, and a select few boys, after years of apprenticeship, made it to the lofty position of roller. Craig became a roller, but "gender was the big thing," said Roxanne. "I could not overcome that."

"There was one grill in the basement, one rolling station, four uncles, lots of cigarettes, and lots of beer," said Craig. "The station was down by the old octopus furnace, so it was hot down there, too. The men wore sleeveless white T-shirts, and most of them had a cigarette hanging out of their mouth."

"Did any ash drop in the dough?" I asked.

"Plenty," said Craig.

"I'm sure we were told the dark spots on the lefse were from the griddle, not the ash," said Roxanne.

"I'm getting the picture there was not much mirth while making lefse," I said.

"There was *no* mirth downstairs; there was a lot of control," said Roxanne. "The women upstairs would be laughing because it was potatoes, after all. All you had to do was get dough downstairs in time for the next round. Still, you couldn't get too lax upstairs because the keepers of the lefse were downstairs. And Lord help you if you tried to eat lefse that day. It was just forbidden. You would get the glance. You learned very young that this was about making lefse."

The mirthless lefse making got to be too much, and the annual gathering stopped. Folks lost interest as they aged, married, and went their separate ways. Then one Christmas in the 1980s, Roxanne and Craig gave each other a potato ricer, hoping to spark interest in lefse making. They each bought a grill and started making lefse separately. Then they made it with other family members, and then with family and friends.

"But again, we were into *making* lefse but forbidding anyone from eating it," said Roxanne. "*That* was a great time! And the competition! There was competition about who could roll the thinnest and the roundest. It became an observed sport rather than a group-participation activity. But there was a bunch of food and everybody would leave with lefse, because that's what we knew."

"So let me get this straight," I said. "No lefse eating, lots of competition, and no laughing. Did you ever get to laugh?"

Roxanne thought a moment. "There was the year ..."

"... when we started drinking!" said Nett Hart, Roxanne's sister, who was coaching 6-year-old Sophie Hart, a grandniece, on rolling a round.

"Seriously," said Roxanne, "there was the year when Anna Kraning, who was 5 years old and doing 'understudy' work in the kitchen, came up to us all and said, 'Can I try some?' Nett and I looked at each other, and it was like, *What?!* And Sharon Sinclair, her mom, said, 'Well, sure, let's do it.' Nett and I were like pointers fixed on this scene, and we didn't say no. But the reality of that moment smacked us in the face. It was like, *Oh my gosh!*"

So the gathering moved away from the big event with competition and high production to become "more of an intergenerational thing for the family," said Roxanne. "Around this time I named it the Hart Lefsefest, in part to remind us that we were going to lighten up and have fun, too! It has taken us a few years of trying this. The last two years we only did 5 pounds of potatoes, but in the past we had been doing up to 25. Once we made the breakthrough of limiting how much lefse we

Sophie Hart, 6, takes her turn at rolling during the Hart Lefsefest.

Charlie Hart, 4, demonstrates the "smack and roll." He shouts, "Smack!" as he throws his dough ball on the rolling surface.

did, we started to laugh. There was less focus on *making*, and more on fun and family."

The family was a mix of Germans, Brits, Finns, Swedes, and Norskies, so I asked why they kept up this Norwegian tradition of making lefse.

"Easy," said Nett. "Just to be together. The whole family comes together."

"Other than lefse making," said John Hart, one of Craig's sons, "I would not want to hang out with any of you guys!"

"Well, then when you come," said Nett, "we don't talk to you."

"I like to make jokes," said John.

"And we're still waiting to hear a good one!" said Anndrea Brand, Craig's fiancée.

"It's nice having *some* tradition within the family," said Roxanne. "Because things can get pretty fragmented, and we are all independent by nature. So to have one thing, lefse making, that people can count on and look forward to is important."

Lefse, Family, Friends, Fun

Lefse fests are like barn raisings: lots of effort; lots of family, friends, and fun; and lots of fulfillment. They are irresistible

Lefse making is all about family time. Below, my family 25 years ago. Above, I'm holding the ricer and, left to right, are Ben Legwold (son), Kate McIntosh (daughter), Amaya McIntosh (granddaughter), Jane Legwold (wife), and Zo McIntosh (grandson).

and irreplaceable as a way of bringing the gang together and reconnecting over rolling pins and delicious rounds of lefse. For Scandinavians and others, lefse fests are the surest way to get all generations out of their silos and into "a *whee* of a time," as Karen Mattson of Austin, Minnesota, described her 12-member overnight lefse fest.

As for me, I learn from every lefse maker I meet and every lefse fest I attend. For example, I learned from the Harts that you have to focus on fun and not be distracted by production or perfect lefse. People at the Hart Lefsefest were making every mistake possible in terms of rolling and grilling. So? If this weren't about fun, 4-year-old Charlie Hart would have never been allowed to pick up a rolling pin—and certainly not permitted to "smack and roll." He'd gleefully shout, "Smack!" as he threw down his dough ball on the rolling surface. Then he'd roll the round with his tongue out and sliding side to side.

I have learned that I want to create my own lefse fest. I want a piece of all that fun! As a lefse maker, I work alone, mostly. Kate, my daughter, and Amaya and Zo, my grandkids, roll a round now and then, but typically I'm a lone roller. I enjoy the solitude, the lefse meditation, but I miss passing on the heritage and the fun of lefse fests. At lefse fests, laughter is the only sound as common as the thumping of rolling pins.

So this fall, I will organize my first lefse fest. I will put out word that extended family members can gather at my place to have fun, learn to make lefse, and take a package home (in that order). Or, because my mentor Linda Bengtson cannot travel to family gatherings anymore, I may suggest we do the lefse fest at her place so she can coach and enjoy as well. My days of rolling all the lefse—and receiving all the glory—for Thanksgiving and Christmas family dinners are done. It's time to pass on this tradition in my own family, just as Linda passed it on to me and as I have coached other folks to do in their families.

The Joy of Lefse

Before closing this chapter, I want to give this joy that goes with lefse its due. It is so fundamental that we may take it for granted. For those of us who have been around lefse all or most of our lives, this joy is always there, like the sky, so it's easy to overlook it. But I am still struck by the words of Jeremy Daniels, co-owner of Gudrun, the lefse-wrap food truck in Portland, Oregon. Jeremy's multicultural heritage (Korean, Chinese, Spanish, black, Filipino, and Cherokee) did not include lefse. "When I first experienced lefse," he said, "it was such a transformative, really spectacular experience. When I tasted it, it seemed like I could have or should have been eating it since I was a little kid. It was so comforting. It was beautiful. Beautiful!"

Not only is his take on lefse beautiful, but there is also beauty in how this Norwegian treat has a universal appeal that blows away ethnic boundaries. That heartens me.

Priscila Agbayani, 56, a Filipino in San Clemente, California, has a story that is all about the joy of lefse. Priscila immigrated to the United States after attending college at the University of Santo Tomas in Manila, Philippines. She began working as an electromechanical engineer. About a dozen years ago, her boss, Kenneth Johnsen, mentioned that he loved lefse and ordered it from a commercial lefse producer in the Midwest because he could not make it or get it locally. She volunteered to give lefse making a try. Lefse was "really hard to make with no tools except a frying pan and rolling pin and bare hands," Priscila told me. "That's all. I had the recipe but no instructions on how to make it. But all I know is I like it. I have to make it."

The result was not great. "Everything was sticking—a disaster," Priscila recalled. Results were the same for several years until Kenneth gave her "a starter toolkit together with a book [*The Last Word on Lefse*], everything I needed to make a

Priscila Agbayani: "Norwegian people, lefse has to pass on. That's all I can say."

good lefse. I said, 'My goodness, no wonder I've been struggling! There is really a way to do it here.' So I kept experimenting with different potatoes and everything. I finally became happy with the result, and I gave one lefse to Kenneth. He said, 'Oh my, this is the best!' In fact, the family did not order any more. Now he keeps on waiting for me to give him some.

"Lefse is like a food of love. It's hard work to make it and you have to have patience, but it's great. It's an amazing experience to make it. I would consider this to be one of the hardest foods I've made, because every time I make it I have to set aside the whole day to make it and clean the kitchen. It's a big challenge, but after making it and eating it, it's such an accomplishment. You really have to be into it. You really have to love it. It's a joy, that's how I feel. I accomplished this thing, and I look at it after I put it on the counter, and I think, *Oh my gosh, here we go again!*"

In an email, Priscila told me she was making lefse for a party at the office of her husband, Ferdinand Agbayani. "I am happy," she said, "because he wants to introduce the Norwegian delicious lefse to other people, to the Vietnamese, Indian, Chinese, Thai, Indonesian, Greek, and Iranian people at his work. I am pretty sure I will receive texts or emails from them, asking for the recipe."

Priscila taught lefse making to her daughter, Kyla, and to Kenneth's niece, Melissa Johnsen, who "has the blood and the heritage—she should learn," said Priscila. "If you have Norwegian heritage, lefse is a treasure to pass on to the next generation. It's so good. It's a big honor to be able to share this with different people. You should spread the word. I know it's from Norway and exclusively originated from them, but it's nice to share it with all kinds of people. Norwegian people, lefse has to pass on. That's all I can say."

Don't let traditions die. Traditions are important, and family get-togethers are important. Lefse making is a family activity that we lived with— and that still brings families together today.

—Brenda Brown, 53, St. Francis, Minnesota

Biddy Seim's hands are cramped by arthritis, but she says, "Have I thought about stopping the lefse making? Not really."

THE BETTER BIDDY

You can employ the word *biddy* two ways:
1. Use it to describe a fussy, mean, gossipy busybody, as in "old biddy."
2. Name someone Biddy. You may remember Biddy from *Great Expectations,* by Charles Dickens. Biddy was the kindhearted country girl who befriended Pip in school and later in life when Pip was in need.

Well—based on what I observed one day as she made lefse on her farm seven miles south of Detroit Lakes, Minnesota—Biddy Seim couldn't be mean even if you stomped on her sandbakkles. Besides, she's only 89, and she rolls lefse. So, no, "old biddy" doesn't fit. But naming this kindhearted country girl Biddy? Yep, that is spot-on.

As Biddy rolled out a round, I noticed her hands. When her son Steve Seim emailed me to suggest Biddy for an interview, he wrote, "I could send you a picture of her hands, and you would be amazed that she could do *anything.*"

I asked Biddy about the arthritis. "You do what you have to

do," she said as she used a neon pink feather duster to brush excess flour off the lefse. "You just kinda work around it. Have I thought about stopping the lefse making? Not really. Some things are harder to do. Certain things you have to live with. I've had open-heart surgery, a mastectomy, my hips redone, and operations on my feet. But I'm not going to stop just because it gets a little harder. Lefse making is just something we do."

Biddy is half Swedish, and the rest is German, Welsh, Irish, and Scottish. Biddy had 11 children with Elmer Seim, 95. "Dad's [Elmer's] the full Norwegian. I'm a duke's mixture," she quipped. "But that's what they say about dogs: Mix breeds are the best ones.

"My mother never made lefse. I remember going to a neighbor's as a 6- or 7-year-old kid. She had a big black stove and was making lefse. I went home and told my mother that Mrs. Lynch was making big pancakes on top of her stove. I didn't know what it was, but it looked like pancakes."

Elmer got up from his nap. He was the classic Norwegian: good-looking and slow to speak. But once he got going, he got into it. According to Lee Seim, the eldest son, Elmer was "born on Christmas Day and has complained about it ever since." Elmer and Biddy make a handsome couple.

Biddy's benediction: "Lefse making has its ups and downs, just like life. I mean, you might try to achieve certain things, and then there's a turn in the road. Things come out a little bit different. But in the end, it turns out OK."

Elmer, 95, and Biddy Seim, 89, still host their family lefse fest.

Part 3
Final Rounds

19
It's a Wrap—A Lefse Wrap!

Lefse was a staple. Whenever there were leftover potatoes, my mother, Gudrun Haugen, would make lefse on a wood-burning stove. We probably had lefse close to 365 days a year.

—Cordell Keith Haugen, 76, Nuuanu Valley, Hawaii

I was wrapped in warm feelings when I returned from touring Gudrun, the lefse-wrap food truck in Portland, Oregon. Not only are co-owners Megan Walhood and Jeremy Daniels talented and imaginative—they're doing really cool things with Viking Soul Food—but also they are downright inspiring on two fronts.

First, I could listen to Jeremy talk lefse all day. "I'll zen out while rolling," he said. "It's a good two hours when I kinda think to myself. Once you do it as proficiently as we do—kind of in this robot mode—you can just go at it and think, and it's very comforting. At the same time, there's something wonderful about trying your hardest on this really delicate product. It's not about manhandling it; it's about finesse. I love that."

Second, Megan and Jeremy got me pumped about using lefse wraps to extend the lefse season beyond the holidays. I love the stuff so much that it's hard to see the lefse stage go dark on December 26. Megan and Jeremy made me realize I don't have to say, *"Ha det bra!"* to lefse. I can do lefse wraps instead. I can make them for my own enjoyment, and I can host lefse-wrap parties. What better way to shorten a long winter and extend the time to enjoy lefse?

Original Recipes

The first challenge in planning lefse-wrap parties was to come up with a half dozen or so enticing recipes. I recruited Merritt Campbell, a chef at the Lakewinds Food Co-op in Richfield, Minnesota, to devise both savory and sweet wraps. The task was right in Merritt's wheelhouse; she has spent a lifetime preparing delicacies at country clubs, gourmet grocery stores, and restaurants in the United States and the Virgin Islands. And for the last 10 years, Merritt has enjoyed preparing dishes for entertainers at the Minnesota State Fair. Merritt made quick work of creating the 12 recipes below.

Next I needed a team of taste testers. I didn't want to publish ho-hum lefse-wrap recipes; I only wanted recipes that tasted great to those who know lefse. So I sent out invitations to friends and neighbors, promising professionally prepared lefse wraps and wine. I had a dozen volunteers, just like that. We came up with dates for three parties, and the plan was to test four recipes per party. The taste testers agreed to provide written feedback and offer a witty title for each wrap. Many good suggestions emerged, which meant I had to make a tough call for each recipe title. I managed. Taste testers were also free to suggest original recipes of their own, and for the last party, Merritt used parts of their recipes in her creations.

In the week before each party, I would meet with Merritt and my daughter, Kate McIntosh, who cooks with Merritt at Lakewinds. We would come up with a shopping list for an hors d'oeuvres wrap, a veggie wrap, a meat wrap, and a dessert wrap. I did the shopping, and they did the cooking the day before and the day of the party. I made the lefse the day before each party.

Making Lefse-Wrap Lefse

Making lefse is one thing; making lefse-wrap lefse is another, I discovered. My head told me to make them thicker than normal because I knew they had to be strong enough to hold all the mouthwatering goodies. But my hands would not listen as I rolled. After years of rolling lefse with "thin is in" as my mantra, I could not change my ways for the first lefse-wrap party. In fact, the only complaint in the feedback forms for that first gathering was that some of the wraps leaked. "The sauce found my fingers," was how Pat Layton of Golden Valley, Minnesota, delicately put it.

My mantra for rolling lefse for the second party was "thicker and quicker." If I rolled each round thicker, they would be stronger and less leaky—and the rolling would be quicker because I wouldn't have to make so many passes with my pin to get each round thin. This mantra worked, usually, but it took supreme concentration to override the habit built into my hands. I apologized to the taste testers for those lefse that still came out thin—was *that* weird—but stated, rather immodestly, that "asking me to make thick lefse was like asking Pavarotti to sing off-key."

So, try to make your lefse-wrap rounds thicker than you normally roll lefse. However, if you fail to make thick lefse, don't worry too much about it. You can always double up two thin lefse to make your wraps, which was the suggestion of taste tester Leila Mikkelson Preston of Brandon, Minnesota. Also, you can serve the wraps on a plate and with a fork. If the lefse tears and the handheld

Chef Merritt Campbell created 12 recipes for three lefse-wrap parties.

Lefse-wrap party taste testers, seated, from left: Leila Mikkelson Preston, Mary Kay Willert, Merritt Campbell, Kate McIntosh, Amaya McIntosh. Standing, from left: John Ziegenhagen, Claude Riedel, Dennis Preston, Paul Olson, me, David Linder, Laurel Riedel.

wrap leaks, it still tastes great from the plate. After all, lefse adds so much to the flavor of meats, veggies, sauces, and sweets. It is pretty and potato-y, and "a calm base to the multi-textured fillings with zesty flavors," said Claude Riedel of Minneapolis.

Most other types of wraps have wrappings that add no taste—zilch. Megan Walhood said most non-lefse wrappings "could be cardboard. You don't want to use just any old starch vehicle to put your food in. Lefse works conceptually because there is universality to taking some kind of starch [and lefse is some kind of starch] and putting fillings inside. Sandwiches, gyros, every culture has some version of what this is. So a lefse wrap isn't really that radical."

I should add that for each party I made a small batch of gluten-free lefse for two taste testers. While they were appreciative and glad they could partake in the party, I was not entirely satisfied with the gluten-free lefse I made. I used a recipe with gluten-free flour and xanthan gum, which is a thickening agent that helps replace gluten and therefore hold the lefse round together. But the lefse turned out drier and grittier than lefse made with regular flour, and the edges of the rounds tended to be more ragged. I know there must be good recipes out there, but I just have not found one as of this writing.

Party tip: Have a stack of lefse at the ready for those who like all the exciting flavors at the party but are in need of a pure lefse fix. Paul Olson of Minneapolis said after eating one lefse wrap, "I ate a little lefse that was left behind, and that gave everything a nice aftertaste."

Here are the ingredients and instructions for Merritt's 12 wraps. Each wrap serves four partygoers. Each lefse round should have a 12- to 14-inch diameter.

Lefse Wraps Party #1

ELECTRO-LOX
Smoked salmon lefse wrap

8	ounces softened cream cheese
8	ounces sliced smoked salmon
1	red onion, minced
2	ounces capers

Spread softened cream cheese on 4 rounds of lefse. Lay smoked salmon on cream cheese. Sprinkle with minced onions and capers. Roll lefse and cut into pinwheels.

SKOGEN'S SOPP (THE FOREST'S MUSHROOM)

Mushrooms in gjetost sauce lefse wrap

3	tablespoons olive oil
1	large yellow onion, chopped
4	pints button, cremini, shiitake, or portabella mushrooms, sliced
1	teaspoon thyme
1	teaspoon black pepper
4	tablespoons butter
¼	cup flour
2	cups milk
½	cup white wine
12	ounces grated gjetost cheese
¼	teaspoon grated nutmeg
	salt

Heat oil in large skillet until shimmering. Add onions and sauté until translucent. Add sliced mushrooms, thyme, and pepper, and sauté until soft. Set aside.

In saucepan, melt butter and whisk in flour a little at a time. Whisk until there are no lumps, then cook roux until golden brown. Add milk a little at a time, whisking to avoid lumps. Stir constantly until mixture thickens. Add white wine, grated gjetost, and nutmeg. Stir until cheese melts. Add salt to taste.

Add enough of the cheese sauce to mushroom mixture to make a moist-but-solid wrap mixture. Lay out 4 lefse and spoon the filling on a line along the diameter of each round, leaving 2 inches from the edge on both sides free of filling. Flip one side of the round over the filling, fold the two ends in, and continue to roll the wrap, burrito-style.

A TASTE OF HEAVEN
Skillet supper lefse wrap

2   tablespoons olive oil
1   red onion, thinly sliced
1   pound hot or mild ground Italian sausage
3   tablespoons apple cider vinegar
3   tablespoons light brown sugar
2   apples, thinly sliced
½   small head purple cabbage, thinly sliced

Heat olive oil and sauté onion until translucent. Add crumbled Italian sausage and cook through. Drain excess oil from onion-sausage mixture. Add cider vinegar and brown sugar, and mix well. Add apple slices to mixture, and sauté until slices begin to soften. Add cabbage and cook until it begins to soften but is still crunchy.

Lay out 4 lefse, and add a line of sausage mixture across the diameter of each round. Roll lefse burrito-style, and cut in half.

BERRY, BERRY NORSK
Berry-stuffed lefse wrap

½   pint blueberries
½   pint raspberries
½   pint sliced strawberries
8   ounces softened cream cheese
¼   cup granulated sugar
1   teaspoon vanilla

Combine berries and set aside.

In mixer or by hand, whip cream cheese. Add sugar and vanilla and combine well. Spread sweetened cream cheese on 4 lefse. Add a line of berry mixture across the diameter of each lefse, and roll burrito-style.

Lefse Wraps Party #2

Shrimp lefse rollup.

SHRIMP IN A BLANKET
Shrimp lefse rollup

8	ounces softened cream cheese
4	ounces shrimp-cocktail sauce
12	ounces peeled, deveined, cooked shrimp (recommend 21 to 25 count shrimp, each cut in two or three pieces, for 4 rounds of lefse)
¼	cup chopped parsley

Spread softened cream cheese on 4 rounds of lefse. Spread cocktail sauce over cream cheese. Sprinkle shrimp pieces all over cocktail sauce. Sprinkle parsley over all. Roll up lefse, and cut into pinwheels.

Barbecued-beef lefse wrap.

NORSK RODEO IN MINNESOTA HEAT
Barbecued-beef lefse wrap

2	tablespoons cooking oil		1	cup rice vinegar
3	pounds chuck roast		½	cup sugar
4	cups beef stock		½	teaspoon red pepper flakes
1	yellow onion, quartered		½	small head green cabbage, shredded
6	cloves garlic		8	ounces shredded carrots (about 1 cup)
12	ounces ginger ale		1	bunch radishes, sliced
12	ounces barbecue sauce		1	small yellow onion, sliced

Preheat oven to 350 degrees. In large ovenproof casserole, heat oil and brown beef. Add beef stock, quartered onion, and garlic cloves. Roast in oven, covered, 2 to 3 hours, until meat starts to pull apart when prodded with a fork. Drain beef stock from pan. Mix together ginger ale and barbecue sauce and add to casserole. Continue roasting, covered, for another hour.

Meanwhile, mix rice vinegar, sugar, and red pepper flakes. Add shredded cabbage, shredded carrots, sliced radishes, and sliced onion to vinegar mix. Set aside to marinate until veggies soften slightly.

Remove beef from oven and cool slightly. Pull apart beef with a pair of forks. Place beef in bowl and add enough of the barbecue sauce–ginger ale mix to moisten meat thoroughly.

Drain vegetables.

Lay out 4 lefse rounds. Spread a line of beef mixture across the diameter of each lefse. Top with a line of crunchy vegetables. Roll burrito-style.

EAT YOUR VEGGIES, OLE!
Eggplant-and-tomato lefse wrap

2	medium eggplants, peeled and cut in ¾-inch cubes
4	tablespoons olive oil, divided
	salt, to sprinkle
	oregano, to sprinkle
	granulated garlic, to sprinkle
1	pint grape tomatoes
	tarragon, to sprinkle
	basil, to sprinkle
8	ounces plain hummus

Preheat oven to 350 degrees. In mixing bowl, toss eggplant in half the olive oil. Sprinkle with salt, oregano, and granulated garlic. Place on rimmed baking sheet.

In another mixing bowl, toss grape tomatoes in remaining olive oil. Sprinkle with salt, granulated garlic, tarragon, and basil. Place on separate rimmed baking sheet.

Roast vegetables at same time on separate racks. Roast tomatoes until softened and juicy, about 15 to 18 minutes. Roast eggplant for 18 to 20 minutes, until a little browned on edges. Combine roasted eggplant and tomatoes.

Spread 4 rounds of lefse with hummus. Place a row of vegetable mixture across the diameter of each lefse. Roll burrito-style.

APPLE LENA LEFSE
Caramel apple crumble lefse wrap

1	cup flour	1	cup cream
1	cup oatmeal	4	apples, thinly sliced
2	cups packed light		(use good cooking
	brown sugar, divided		apples like Granny
1	teaspoon ground		Smith or Braeburn)
	ginger	2	tablespoons
1	teaspoon cinnamon		cinnamon sugar
16	tablespoons cold	½	cup chopped pecans
	butter, divided		

To prepare crumble: In food processor, mix flour, oatmeal, 1 cup brown sugar, ginger, cinnamon, and 8 tablespoons cold butter cut in pieces. Pulse until a crumble forms. Set aside.

To prepare caramel sauce: Melt remaining 8 tablespoons butter in saucepan. Add remaining 1 cup brown sugar and bring to boil, stirring often. When boiling vigorously, pour in cream. Stir until caramel comes together. Set aside.

To prepare apples: Add 2 tablespoons water to a skillet, then add apple slices and cinnamon sugar. Cook until apples start to soften.

Lay out 4 lefse rounds. Put apples in a line on the diameter of each lefse. Sprinkle with crumble, pecans, and a generous amount of caramel. Roll burrito-style.

Caramel apple crumble lefse wrap.

Lefse Wraps Party #3

HAMLET AND A PICKLE
Danish ham-and-cheese lefse wrap

4   tablespoons stone-ground mustard
1   pound thinly sliced Danish ham
¾   pound thinly sliced Havarti cheese
8   crisp kosher dill pickle spears

Spread 4 lefse rounds with stone-ground mustard. Cover lefse with a layer of ham, and then cover with a layer of cheese. Lay two pickle spears across the diameter of each lefse. Roll up lefse and cut into pinwheels.

Danish ham-and-cheese lefse wrap.

Sweet-potato salad lefse wrap.

FRESHA LEFSE VEGGIE WRAP
Sweet-potato salad lefse wrap

1	cup rice vinegar
¾	cup packed light brown sugar
1	teaspoon sesame oil
1	teaspoon ground ginger
¼	teaspoon cayenne
2	large sweet potatoes, peeled and cut into ¾-inch cubes
3	stalks celery, chopped
1	small red onion, chopped
½	bunch cilantro, finely chopped

Mix vinegar, brown sugar, sesame oil, ginger, and cayenne. Set aside.

Boil sweet potato cubes until cooked but still firm; drain. Pour dressing over hot potatoes. When potatoes are cool, add celery, onion, and cilantro, and toss together. Drain excess dressing from salad, and place salad in line on the diameter of 4 lefse rounds. Roll burrito-style.

LENA HAD A LITTLE LAMB
Lamb-filled lefse wrap

2	tablespoons cooking oil	3	tablespoons tomato paste
1	yellow onion, chopped	2	ripe tomatoes, chopped
2	cloves garlic, minced	1	zucchini, chopped
1	pound ground lamb	3	tablespoons chopped parsley
1	tablespoon paprika	¼	cup chopped pistachios
2	teaspoons ground cumin		
1	teaspoon salt		
1½	teaspoons black pepper		

Heat oil in skillet. Sauté onion until translucent. Add minced garlic. Crumble ground lamb into skillet and brown. Add paprika, cumin, salt, and pepper, stirring occasionally until lamb is cooked through. Drain excess oil. Add tomato paste to mixture and stir well. Add tomatoes and zucchini, and cook until zucchini begins to soften.

Spread lamb mixture in a line on the diameter of 4 lefse rounds. Sprinkle with parsley and pistachios. Roll burrito-style.

Lamb-filled lefse wrap.

Chocolate-banana lefse wrap.

THE AMEN LEFSE
Chocolate-banana lefse wrap

2	ounces unsweetened chocolate	¼	cup cocoa powder
4	tablespoons butter	½	cup cream
¾	cup sugar	6	ripe bananas
		½	cup chopped pecans

To prepare fudge sauce: Melt chocolate and butter in a double boiler. Stir in sugar, cocoa, and cream. Cook over low heat for 15 to 20 minutes, stirring occasionally until smooth. Set aside.

Slice bananas and spread in a line on the diameter of 4 lefse rounds. Drizzle generously with fudge sauce, and sprinkle with pecans. Roll burrito-style.

*Sharon, my wife who passed in 2013,
used to go to a Celiac-disease support group
in Brainerd. Before each holiday, the ladies used
to bring in their gluten-free baked items
and casseroles. I went to the meeting once and
took three dozen of my gluten-free lefse.
There are lots of Norwegians and Swedes in the
territory, and a lot of people like me—
I'm German-Irish—who love lefse. There was one
elderly woman there named Betty, and when
I walked in with that gluten-free lefse,
Betty said, "Is that lefse?" I said, "Yes, Betty,
this is lefse." Tears ran down her cheeks,
and she said, "I never thought I would
have lefse again!"*

–Nolan Spencer, 77, Deerwood, Minnesota

RECIPE THAT LAUNCHED THE LEFSE-WRAP FOOD TRUCK

Here is the recipe for Norwegian meatballs in caramelized goat cheese (gjetost) gravy, served with sweet-and-sour cabbage. This is the signature lefse wrap of Viking Soul Food, the lefse-wrap food truck in Portland, Oregon. Co-owners Megan Walhood and Jeremy Daniels generously shared it with me.

Norwegian meatballs in caramelized goat cheese (gjetost) gravy, served with sweet-and-sour cabbage.

GJETOST SAUCE
Caramalized goat cheese gravy

You will need a sturdy whisk and a wand immersion blender. These tools really help if you decide to double or triple the batch to feed a large group.

8	tablespoons butter
½	cup flour
4	cups whole milk, divided
½	cup Madeira wine
½	cup white wine
6	ounces grated gjetost
½	teaspoon freshly grated nutmeg
1-2	teaspoons salt

In a large pot, melt the butter on medium-high heat until no longer steaming. To minimize lumps in the sauce, remove as much moisture as possible from the butter before adding flour, which can also contain moisture.

Add flour and whisk until a smooth paste forms. Check every 5 minutes to ensure the roux isn't burning. Continue cooking until roux is about the same color as the gjetost, a caramel brown.

Liquids are next. The order in which liquids are added to the pot is crucial to prevent lumps, so be sure to follow closely.

Pour 2 cups milk into the pot, then put the immersion blender in the pot and turn the blender on low. Position the blender vertically, and drag it along the bottom of the pot to ensure it blends all the flour. Continue blending until you're convinced there are no lumps. Let this mixture fully incorporate and thicken before adding the remaining

2 cups milk. Add the Madeira and the white wine. Use the sturdy whisk to whisk like mad. Then use the immersion blender to make sure things come back together as one silky, smooth sauce. Cook on medium-low until the sauce comes to a boil and begins to thicken.

Stir in grated gjetost, nutmeg, and salt.

Two options for finishing the sauce:
Fast. Stand over the pot, crank up heat to high, and whisk-blend–alternating between the whisk and the blender–until the sauce comes up to a boil. Continue whisking constantly until sauce is thickened. Be careful not to burn the bottom.
Not so fast. Turn heat down to low. Whisk sauce every 15 minutes, scraping along the bottom to make sure you've got no lumps or burned areas. The sauce should come only to a simmer.

The sauce is done when nicely thickened and all raw flour taste has cooked out.

Whichever method you choose, give the sauce a taste test and season with salt and pepper as needed. Then finish the sauce with a thorough immersion wand blending.

NORWEGIAN MEATBALLS
Viking Soul Food style

2	slices Scandinavian-style sourdough rye bread (a dense seeded bread made with 100-percent rye flour; KrustaVita is a good brand)
3	tablespoons heavy cream
3	tablespoons whole milk

4	organic eggs
2	tablespoons flour
½	tablespoon allspice berries, ground
1	teaspoon black peppercorns, ground
1	tablespoon caramelized onions (finely diced onions slowly cooked in butter with salt until very dark brown; Viking Soul Food makes large batches of caramelized onions and freezes them for various applications)
2	teaspoons kosher salt
1	pound ground pork, preferably free of hormones and antibiotics
1	pound ground beef, preferably grass-fed

For the rye bread: Use a food processor to pulse bread to crumbs. Mix crumbs with cream and milk.

For the meatballs: Mix together bread crumb mixture and remaining ingredients except meat, then incorporate meat, squeezing with your fingers to make sure starchy ingredients break up in the meat. Let stand at least 2 to 3 hours in refrigerator before rolling into 1-inch balls.

Preheat oven to 500 degrees and bake meatballs for about 9 minutes or until they are medium-rare in the middle and just beginning to brown on the outside.

Add meatballs to slow cooker set on warm/low or to large pot set on warm/simmer. Pour gjetost sauce over the top, and finish cooking meatballs for another 30 to 45 minutes.

SURKAL
Sweet-and-sour cabbage with caraway

A classic Norwegian side dish. The traditional recipe for surkal involves cooking the cabbage for over an hour until soft, but we wanted some crunch, so we altered it a bit to suit our needs. Our version is also nonfat.

- ½ **cup red wine vinegar**
- ½ **cup apple cider vinegar**
- 1 **cup water**
- 1 **cup sugar**
- ¼ **cup kosher salt**
- 2 **teaspoons caraway seeds**
- 1 **bay leaf**
- 1 **small head red cabbage, cored and thinly sliced**

In a pot, add everything but the cabbage. Bring to a boil, then reduce heat to a low simmer for 10 minutes. Pour mixture over the chopped cabbage and allow to sit at room temperature for a day before serving. Surkal will keep for months in the refrigerator.

MAKING THE LEFSE WRAP

Warm a lefse round on a hot griddle, and then lay it on a plate. Spread about ½ cup of surkal in a line on the diameter of the lefse. Top with 2 or 3 of the meatballs and a generous amount of the gjetost sauce. Roll burrito-style.

Optional upgrade: Add 1 to 2 teaspoons of lingonberry preserves before wrapping your lefse.

20
Make an Heirloom Lefse Rolling Pin

Three Christmases ago, I was told that I had to open the first present. We usually don't do something like this, but I said OK. A lot of cameras were at the ready, and when I opened the present, it was my grandmother Myrtle's lefse rolling pin. She used to wrap her pin in tinfoil, not a sock, to prevent the flour from getting in the grooves. My dad said that I might as well have it, and so I have two pins now. That was very neat.

—Dave Glomstad, 53, La Crescent, Minnesota

There is something holy in an old lefse rolling pin. It has to do with the sense of touch, with those saintly hands that made the handles shine. With the intimacy and the functional friendship that the pin provides, a woman or a man can roll lefse in a slice of solitude leading up to the most festive time of the year. Or if the pin is really an antique, the holiness has to do with stories the wood harbors: tales of rolling in Norway and finding its way across the ocean to the United States.

I've always regretted that Grandma Jennie Legwold's rolling pin is lost, perhaps sold with other kitchen tools in a box at her estate sale. From my maternal grandma, Elsie Gehring, I have a blue ceramic mixing bowl. Inherited from my mother, Darlene Schumacher, that chipped and cracked blue bowl warms my heart each time I make lefse, and it graces the cover of this book. But oh how I wish I could roll with Grandma Legwold's lefse pin.

Handles So Smooth

Is it a sin
To covet a pin
That rolls
A round of lefse?

No, it's OK
To want in your way,
For pins
Hold a nana's touch.

Handles so smooth,
Chips in their grooves,
Their trail

Is the lace of love.

Since I cannot roll with the memories tactilely stimulated by Grandma Legwold's rolling pin, I roll with a Bethany rolling pin. It is reasonably priced and reliable, but it is not special. It's the same kind of pin that thousands of others use. Is that the pin I want to pass on to my children?

It's doable! You can make heirloom lefse rolling pins and a lefse stick like these made by Minnesota Woodturners Association members.

In the Presence of Special Pins

To me, the best reason to visit Vesterheim Norwegian-American Museum in Decorah, Iowa, is to see and hold the venerable, heirloom rolling pins. The fact that they are in a museum speaks to lefse's status in the Scandinavian culture. Not only did most of these pins pound out a lot of lefse—in a few cases, the grooves are almost worn away—but they were also beautifully handcrafted. They are sculptures.

One lefse pin remains in my memory from researching *The Last Word on Lefse*: the pin of Alice Miller of Story City, Iowa. "Alice had the most beautiful lefse pin I had ever seen," I wrote. "Made of walnut in Norway about a hundred years ago, it was dark and strong. The white flour in the grooves made the grain in the walnut come to life. A deep gnarly flour-filled groove twined around one end of the pin out into the fixed smoothed handle. At first this looked like a serious flaw in the wood, a wound. But as my fingers explored the groove, I wondered if lightning had struck that handle years ago and some of the charge had remained. Alice rolled rhythmically with her pin, and said while making lefse she often remembered her parents and the huge Christmas Eve family gatherings."

Recalling Alice's pin made me ponder making one in my home workshop. But how? How could I produce a pin that is functional as well as beautiful, something I would be proud to pass on to the generations that will follow in my family?

An Heirloom Awaits!

The Lefse Committee
Said make a pin pretty.
It's in
Your gifted hands.

So such is my fate
For me to create
A gift.
An heirloom awaits!

A Sculptor's Lefse Pin

I took my quest to friend and Minneapolis sculptor Paul Olson. In his creative mind, Paul instantly saw a lefse-pin sculpture that was *vertical*, not horizontal, as I had expected. He went to work on his idea and a couple of weeks later presented a rolling-pin sculpture to me over breakfast.

"The woods are walnut, cherry, maple, wenge, and bubinga," said Paul. "I glued these pieces together to form a 3¼-by-3¼-by-10-inch block."

Minneapolis sculptor
Paul Olson's lefse pin.

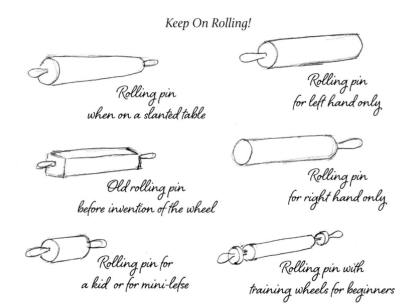

Rolling pin
when on a slanted table

Rolling pin
for left hand only

Old rolling pin
before invention of the wheel

Rolling pin
for right hand only

Rolling pin for
a kid or for mini-lefse

Rolling pin with
training wheels for beginners

Ah, the creative mind! Paul Olson's sketches for lefse pins show design options.

"How did you make the block round?" I asked.

"It's not truly round, but close," he said. "I carved the block into a roughly cylindrical form, using carving teeth attached to a mini-grinder. Then I used a sander to get the finished cylindrical form. I started with grit #36 and ended with grit #220. The cylinder is finished with walnut oil."

"What about the handles?"

"I cut the handles from the legs of an old piece of furniture, and used double-ended dowel screws to attach the handles to the cylinder," he said. "I made the stand from a piece of oak, drilling a hole so the handle fits snugly."

As a bonus, Paul unleashed his humor and drew six other designs for lefse rolling pins. I love his concept for a rolling pin with training wheels for beginners.

While this beautiful piece of art could function as a lefse rolling pin, it lacked grooves that traditional lefse pins have. I asked why, and Paul said the grooves would detract from the look of the piece. "To get grooves, you really need a lathe," he added. "Talk to a woodturner."

Lefse Rolling Pin Contest

I contacted Rick Auge, president of the Minnesota Woodturners Association (MWA). When I told him of my quest, he said his members commonly turn rolling pins. In fact, member Tim Heil once made 76 rolling pins over four months.

A few weeks after contacting Rick, I interviewed Tim in his shop in St. Paul. When I asked why he made *76 rolling pins*, he smiled and said, "I could have stopped at 20, but then I would have wondered: 'How much better would number 21 have been?'"

Sensing woodturners are a special lot, passionate about creating beauty from blocks of wood, I wanted to tap into their energy. I had an idea that I ran past Rick: a Lefse Rolling Pin Contest for MWA members. He liked the idea and suggested I come to their next meeting and roll it out to the membership.

At the June meeting, Rick gave me five minutes to speak to the 80-some members attending. I explained I was writing *Keep On Rolling,* and some of my readers may want to make an heirloom lefse rolling pin. I asked for their help in showing that such a thing could be done by entering my Lefse Rolling Pin Contest. The goal was to turn a lefse rolling pin that was functional as well as artful. The contest would

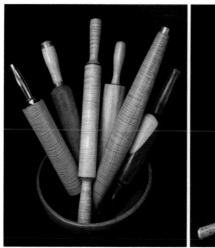

Minnesota woodturners crafted rolling pins for my contest to create the most artful and functional lefse rolling pin.

Jacqui Baker is in her shop where she created the third-place pin.

Jeff Luedloff tied for third with his design of autumn leaves burned on the barrel of his pin.

end at the October meeting, when the winner would receive $500. The second-place winner would get $250, and the third-place prize would be $150. Winners would keep their rolling pins.

Fast forward to October. I had no idea what the response to the contest would be. I knew the prizes were substantial, but would the members skip the contest, thinking an artful lefse-pin project too frilly? Or would they take up the challenge and release their considerable creative powers to make stunning lefse pins? A couple of weeks before the meeting, Rick told me he had not heard of much activity related to the contest, so I was hoping to at least get a few pins, enough to be able to award three prizes.

I was so curious to see the contest entries that I arrived about an hour before the meeting started, just so I could inspect and (hopefully) admire each pin as it was gently placed on the judging table. When I entered the MWA meeting at the Houck Machine Company's shop, I could see through a wide window to a room with a lot of people milling around tables. This is probably common, I thought, because there would be a membership table and perhaps tables for vendors hawking woodturning products and instructional materials. But then a clot of members drifted away from a table that was already full of rolling pins. And in the middle of that table was a small plate of folded lefse!

I tried not to beam too much. These pins were what I had imagined—the equal to Alice Miller's walnut lefse rolling pin. And yet they were better than imagined because they were real, right there before me. About half were not traditional grooved lefse pins, but I didn't care. They were all beautiful. Besides, we lefse makers have rolled with non-grooved pins, and not once did the Lefse Patrol knock on our doors.

What struck me about the entries were the delightful and some-times daring designs, the nature-is-art grain of the woods, the blending of contrasting colors, the shiny metal accent pieces, the sensual shapes, and the flawlessly smooth finishes. Three pins had markings that made them look like young muskellunge fish. One of those, called a baguette rolling pin, was wider in the middle and tapered toward the ends; there were no handles. One was made of gray Corian, the same material used to make kitchen countertops. A couple of them featured *spalting,* a form of wood coloration caused by fungi. A couple of

Minnesota woodturners admire entries for the lefse rolling pin contest. Note the lefse and butter.

Kenneth Gustafson made his second-place walnut lefse rolling pin with a lathe purchased for $100.

pins had bold, red bands. The glued woods of two pins spiraled from end to end.

Standing over the judging table, I realized there was good news and bad news. The good news: Making an heirloom-quality rolling pin was doable. Yes, I would have to buy a lathe and woodturning tools, and I would have to take classes and "make chips," the piles of shavings that accompany woodturning. Two weeks after the meeting, I joined the MWA because of the fellowship and the instructional workshops. Learning would take time and practice and attention to detail. If you are interested in making such a pin, check out woodturning associations and clubs near you as well as the American Association of Woodturners, based in St. Paul, Minnesota.

The bad news regarding the contest: I had to choose winners from a table of excellence. I was wise enough to have asked Dan Cary and Rob Johnstone, editors at *Woodworker's Journal*, to join MWA member Janese Evans and me as judges. I figured we'd have strength in numbers, and if things got ugly because of our choices, the four of us could hold off a mutinous lot of non-winners long enough for the police to arrive and aid our escape.

As the general meeting began with announcements and reminders about classes, we judges settled into studying the entries. We worked with the understanding that we might make a bad call. After 10 minutes of hemming and hawing and speaking in hushed tones, we decided there was a tie for third, and we would award $100 to each third-place winner. *Woodworker's Journal* kindly chipped in $50 to the purse. We considered Bob Puetz's pin for third place, but settled on pins by Jacqui Baker of rural Isanti County and Jeff Luedloff of Shakopee. Jacqui's simple-but-elegant design allowed the wood to speak for itself. Jeff's pin was the most original of the lot, with autumnal red and yellow leaves burned on the barrel.

In his woodworking shop, Bob Puetz holds his lefse pin, which finished just out of the money in the contest.

Second place went to Kenneth Gustafson of Princeton. For his traditional grooved lefse pin, Ken chose walnut because he knew, based on my talk in June, that I had a soft spot in my heart for walnut. Good choice. I admit Ken's pin is the one I aspire to make. I also liked his low-key approach to woodturning. "I try something, and if it doesn't turn out, I can just go on to the next hunk of wood," Ken said. He planned to pass on his lefse pin as an heirloom.

And the Winner Is ...

The first-place prize was the easiest to give. The judges unanimously agreed that Dan Larson, of Little Canada, Minnesota, presented the no-doubt winner. Dan opened the floodgates to his reservoir of creative—and competitive—juices for this contest. "I knew I could make a rolling pin," he said a few weeks later when I interviewed him in his shop, "but could I make one that was exceptional?"

For two months after the contest announcement, Dan reflected on how to make his pin stand out. "To get a quality piece," he said, "it's good to slow down and think a long time about design."

Initially, he considered making a pin of glued-together exotic woods. But he nixed the idea. "Everybody's going to be doing that," he said. He played with a few other concepts and then settled on using three woods to make a pin and its stand: spalted birch for the handles, applewood for the stand, and a maple burl for the barrel.

A burl is a rounded, knotty growth on a tree. "When you look inside a piece of wood, you never know what you are going to find, especially with a big maple burl with odd shapes like I had," Dan said. "So you have to be open to whatever comes. If I have one piece of advice for beginners, it's to listen to the wood. Let it have its way."

The first two blocks of the burl gave Dan a lot of back talk as he gouged, scraped, and chiseled to remove layers of wood. These blocks turned out to be unattractive, but the more Dan worked with a third block on his lathe, the more it showed its moody beauty with dark-reddish swirls and brown knots splashed on a blond background. Dan knew he had discovered a winning piece, and he rounded the barrel, created lefse-pin grooves, sanded the wood, and applied a food-safe finish of walnut oil.

Dan had initially intended to narrow the ends of this handsome hunk of heaven to make fixed handles. "But my wife said she wanted a pin she could actually use," said Dan. "She said rolling was better with a pin that had ball bearings in the handles. So I drilled a hole and ran a food-safe stainless-steel axle through the length of the barrel and attached food-safe ball bearings."

Next, he shaped the handles with his lathe and then burned tiny hash marks on each. He also carved and burned thick black lines that twine around the handles. He was inspired by the designs and techniques made famous by Avelino Samuel, a woodturner artist from St. John, U.S. Virgin Islands. "It was a lot of work, but a lot of fun," Dan said.

Dan drilled holes in the handles for the axle, and

Dan Larson shows a burl that may—or may not—hold a woodturner's treasure inside.

Dan Larson's lefse rolling pin won first place.

he hand-sanded and applied finish to each handle. Finally, he assembled all parts of the rolling pin and mounted the pin on an applewood stand, also turned on his lathe.

The evening of the contest, Dan and his wife, Helen Curphey-Larson, were not leaving anything to chance. On a small wooden plate, Dan burned an explanation of the woods used to make the lefse pin, the food-safe finish, and the hidden ball bearings. "And Helen had made some lefse, and so she thought I had better put a little plate of lefse by the pin," said Dan, smiling broadly. "That made sense to me. I mean, if I was going to win the challenge, I was going to have to go all out."

Call it the lefse advantage.

TIP: *I have three different rolling pins. I have two of the regular ones and then a little one that's like a small paint roller. I think that small one is the nicest because it can help make your lefse rounder and it's easy to hold. Using multiple rolling pins is probably a bigger help than any tip I can advise.*

—Janice Knudson Redford, 75, Cambridge, Wisconsin

THE MAKING OF A LEFSE PIN

Eight photos give you an idea how Dan Larson used his lathe to make an heirloom lefse rolling pin. It's doable!

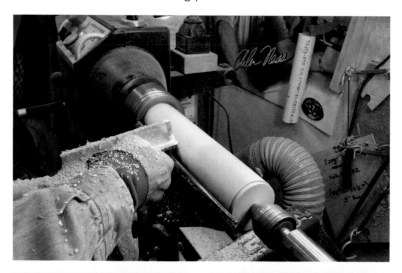

21
The Holy Roller

*When in a storm just let your faith take form/
Keep on a rollin'/The sun will shine anew/So stand
tall, be true, stay strong, be you!*

–lyrics to "Keep On Rollin'"

It was Saturday, July 23, 2016, around 9 a.m., a time when week-enders around Sacred Heart, Minnesota, might be whipping up their waffle batter. But that morning the heavens, which had been steamed and goaded by a mid-July heat wave, furiously flashed a wild thunderbolt at the prairie landscape.

The closest structure to the heavens was a cross atop the tall, graceful steeple of Hawk Creek Lutheran Church. Smoke spewed from the bell tower, gray ghosts streaming straight up to the slate sky. The spirals served as fanfare for the triumphant entrance of malevolent blazes. The orange-skirted steeple, a visual reference point for the region, looked majestic and heroic even as it leaned southward and then crashed to the ground in flames.

Ten fire departments battled the burning for six hours, but the fire destroyed all of the church except for the altar, the baptismal font, and the education wing on the east side.

Four months after that fire, I drove to Sacred Heart on a mission to witness lefse production for Hawk Creek's Lefse Ministry and to interview the church's pastor, the Rev. Dan Bowman, the Holy Roller.

On the two-hour trip from Minneapolis on U.S. 212, I tried to imagine what the 203 members of Hawk Creek lost when fire took the church where they and their ancestors had worshiped since the 1870s. Dan was at the scene when the church burned, and afterward was quoted as saying, "We lost our church building, but we didn't lose a single member of our church—the real church—and that's what really counts for us."

Still, the questions remained: What *was* lost? What did the cherished, open, internal spaces and expansive light and stained glass and vaulted ceilings contribute to sacredness? What could possibly replace the edifice where every member of many families had been baptized and married, where a man could sing for 37 years in the back row of the choir? And what happened to the saints, that "great cloud of witnesses" (Hebrews) who graced and guided the church through the decades?

Lightning struck Hawk Creek Lutheran Church the morning of July 23, 2016, causing most of the building to burn to the ground.

The Rev. Dan Bowman: "My mission field is right here, right here among this Norwegian parish. I needed to learn how to speak their language, and part of their language is their Norwegian heritage. Lefse making just fit right in."

When all of these elements of spiritual life went up in smoke, what remained besides the open land and the rising sun?

Lefse Ministry

Even before Hawk Creek burned down, Pastor Dan had gained small-town fame by connecting faith with lefse. In 2008 he rallied a sleepy congregation to make and sell lefse as a fundraiser. The church slowly grew as the fall grill-and-sell campaigns got bigger and better. Cause and effect? Volunteers made 1,725 rounds to sell and donate that first year, 2,500 the next, and 3,400 each year since 2014. The event evolved from a fundraiser into the Lefse Ministry, with lefse being donated to the Renville Community Thanksgiving Supper, the Granite Falls Lutherans Community Thanksgiving Supper, the Wood Lake Community Christmas Dinner, and needy families in Sacred Heart. The tagline on Hawk Creek's website is now "The Church with the Lefse Ministry."

Part of this ministry includes written material slipped into each lefse package. The material varies: "The Lefse Catechism" was in 2008, "Thanksgiving for Lefse for Thanksgiving" in 2010, "The Lefse Walk" in 2012, "The Ten Words of Lefse" in 2014, and "Table Prayers" in 2016. Another part of the Lefse Ministry involves Dan giving presentations throughout the region. His performance features a lefse sermon and hymns he plays with a saw and a violin bow. (He claims the saw tends to sound "sharp.") The pastor has also developed a lefse liturgy for a worship service with lefse used as communion.

Several years before this trip, I had read "The Lefse Catechism:

A Short Instruction Book of Questions and Answers on the Bible's Message Seen Through Lefse, for All God's Children (Even If You Aren't Norwegian)." Frankly, I didn't know what to make of it. At first blush, I thought Dan's lefse ministry was taking the inspiration of lefse—which can include cornball humor—too far into the realm of faith. In the wrong hands, I thought, a lefse ministry could backfire.

Marilyn Agre, left, and Lois Hegna weigh dough balls with utmost precision.

I still carried this concern as I pulled into the parking lot of the Rock Valle Lutheran Church near Echo, Minnesota, around 11 a.m. This was Hawk Creek's home until new construction was completed on the site of the burned-down church near Sacred Heart, probably by Christmas 2017. The sign along the road in front of Rock Valle said: "A Changeless Christ for a Changing Countryside. Pastor Dan Bowman 9:30 AM."

I opened the door to the church basement, half expecting a dispirited lefse-making crew wearied by grief from the fire. But I had underestimated the power of lefse. I saw white-flour footprints on the blue-gray carpet that covered the stairs. I smelled the toasty aroma of grilling lefse. I heard cheery chatter. All was well.

Fast Rolling, Slow Driving

Dan had a pastor's conference that morning, so I mingled until he arrived around lunchtime. Lois Hegna and Marilyn Agre were weighing dough balls in the basement kitchen, making sure each was between 2.97 and 3.0 ounces. "People were really concerned when the church burned down," said Marilyn. "The first question from just about everyone was, 'Are we still going to be able to

Lowell White, at the Table of the Great Rejecters, packages lefse and inserts table prayers printed on cards.

Marian Froland humbly serves as a quality-control marshal and lefse packager.

have our lefse?' The first year Pastor Dan was here, we didn't have money to pay off our loans. He said he liked to make lefse, and lefse would sell well, that maybe we should have a lefse-making fundraiser. And it went over really well, and we paid off the loans. I think it was something like $5,000."

A wall separated the kitchen from the dining area, where the rolling crew was getting a little rowdy. I asked Lois and Marilyn if they hoped to one day make it to the promised land of rolling and grilling. "Ha! We're grateful to have distance from them," said Lois, chuckling. "It gets crazy out there being around all that flour. We don't roll and fry, so it's good to get together and help otherwise, to be part of the church."

"Plus, we have to make a lot of dough balls," said Marilyn. "When Pastor Dan comes, we have to be ready because he rolls real fast."

I moved on to the dining room, where four 8-foot-long tables were set up for rolling and grilling. Two rolling tables each held two covered pastry boards and were elevated, one by handcrafted plywood stands and the other by black plastic bed risers. The two grilling tables held four traditional electric grills and a dual electric cast-iron commercial crepe maker that was excellent for grilling lefse. Three more tables were draped with cooling towels, and three other tables were for packaging the rounds and inserting "Table Prayers." Loaded with potluck food for the day were three tables in the corner of the basement, away from the production area.

I meandered over to the Table of the Great Rejecters, where Marian Froland and Lowell White humbly served as quality-control marshals and lefse packagers.

"I used to fry," said Marian, "but I had a shoulder replaced and a broken arm. I'm 83. I like a job where I can sit and fold the lefse, and then put three rounds in each bag, which sells for $5."

Lowell also folds after the rounds have cooled. "They gotta be cool," he said, "or they'll stick together when we freeze the packages."

I asked them to evaluate this rolling-and-grilling crew. "Oh, they do all right," said Lowell. "Not very many go into the reject pile. We'll have to brush flour off of some of them. Pastor Bowman makes them too big, and then they are hard to get into the bag."

"When his drape over the edge of the grill, they get crispy," said Marian. "Then we have to use *scissors!*" She pointed to a pile of crisp lefse scraps.

Lisa Neutgens, holding baby Matilda, puts a round on the grill while Orlynn Hegna takes one off.

Like all rollers, Celeste Knutson, in a green T-shirt, works at an elevated table in order to minimize back strain. Also pictured, from left: Mark Bigaouette, Orlynn Hegna, and Joyce Bigaouette.

I asked if they ever told the pastor to roll his rounds smaller.

"Yeah," said Lowell, smiling, "but he doesn't listen."

"And he rolls so much faster than the rest of them, too, you know," added Marian.

"He's a machine," said Lowell.

"He's fast rolling, but he's *so* slow driving," said Marian.

"You've heard about his driving, haven't you?" asked Lowell. "He's got a Prius, and he's in a club trying to get the highest mileage. He drives like 30 miles per hour on the highway. It slows traffic, and cars get backed up on the road."

"He's all for saving money any way he can, you know," said Marian as she folded.

"Even at the parsonage, he'll have the thermostat way down," said Lowell. "That's what I've heard."

"Or else he'll wash clothes in the middle of the night because the electricity is cheaper or something," said Marian.

I walked over to the rolling-and-grilling zone and asked about the pastor's driving. Word was he once got 985 miles on one tank of gas by hypermiling.

"Don't lead Pastor Dan on about this when he gets here," said Liz Lanning, whose job was to feed dough balls to the rollers and transfer the rolled rounds from the pastry board to the grills. "I hate it when I follow him to church. He goes like 23 miles per hour or something. I like to go 55 on the highway."

"The *Amish* are faster than him," said Orlynn Hegna, referring to the Amish mode of getting around: horse and buggy.

The rolling pace was slow because Dan had not yet arrived, so Liz took time to teach her 2-year-old granddaughter, Liddy Neutgens, the art of rolling lefse.

"The Lefse Ministry is wonderful, unique," said Liz. "We know in our hearts we are doing something good for the community. Even though we might not be bringing them to church physically, they are with us in their hearts because they're reading the lefse catechism and the table prayers that we insert in the packages. Where Pastor Dan comes up with these things is amazing to all of us. No one else has ever done it."

While the pastor was away, Celeste Knutson used his rolling pin; hers was squeaking too much for her liking. "Rolling is relaxing," she said. "I'm stiff and sore the next day, in my knees and shoulder, but it's OK. The best part of it is the time we spend here making lefse. I get to know my neighbors. I don't ever get to know them as well as I do during a day rolling lefse. People just want to talk, you know? You're working all day and conversations get going, and you're thankful for that time."

Liz Lanning, left, feeds dough balls to the rollers and transfers rolled rounds from the pastry board to the grills. Pastor Dan, rolling at three pastry boards, keeps her hopping.

Lunch With Dan

Dan arrived and it was time for lunch. Before the group ate, he asked that I read a selection from "Table Prayers." This is the one I chose at random:

Lord, we thank you
For the food before us,
The friends (or family) beside us,
The love between us,
And your presence among us.
Amen

The group ate and talked as I interviewed Dan. I asked about the challenge of getting the Lefse Ministry going. "I was looking for a way we could serve God," he said. "If God provides a way, then we can serve it. When the church questioned if we should do this as a fundraiser, some said yes because we're good at it. Others said no because we should not expect the community to pay our bills.

"So we made 300 lefse for a bazaar and had no rejects—every single round was edible and sellable, which was a big improvement from the bazaar the year before. It was almost a sign from God. So then I thought, 'If we can do this as a ministry instead of as a fundraiser, then it would make sense. Because we could share the gospel through lefse.'"

When he wrote "The Lefse Catechism," he took criticism from colleagues for seeming to make fun of God and religious matters. His response was that Jesus explained spiritual matters using examples from everyday life, and he was trying to do the same using lefse.

"The main thing with the Lefse Ministry is the ingredients used to make lefse are such simple ingredients: flour, butter, sugar, potatoes. Yet together they produce a mouthwatering feast that is going to make any Ole or Lena drool. What does this mean? We are all individuals in the body of Christ. We might be simple little people, yet each one of us has a gift."

Other workers at the table had lingered over empty plates, and conversations had ceased. Dan was holding forth.

"Angels must be passing over; it just got quiet," said festival coordinator Joyce Bigaouette.

"I love rolling lefse," continued Dan. "It's exciting to see people working together, from the youngest child to the oldest member. There's a job for everyone. With a small church that doesn't have a whole lot of programming like a big church does, if people can do something together as a church body, that is significant. It makes a difference in people's lives.

As part of the Lefse Ministry, the Rev. Dan Bowman gives a lefse sermon and leads hymns he plays with a saw and a violin bow. He claims the saw tends to sound "sharp."

"I'm a missionary kid, and I've always wanted to be a missionary. I applied to go into the mission field, and God closed that door. But God has opened my eyes to see that my mission field is right here, right here among this Norwegian parish. I needed to learn how to speak their language, and part of their language is their Norwegian heritage. Lefse making just fit right in."

No one at the table moved, and the angels Joyce had mentioned continued to pass over. It was as if people wanted to bask in the calming-yet-electrifying energy of faith that their pastor was exuding.

After a moment, the angels must have left because a cry came from across the dining room—probably from Liz—to finish eating and get back to work. At 6 feet, 4 inches, Dan, working in a T-shirt at the table placed on the handcrafted stand, used his leverage and what he called a "lefse obsession" to roll with vigor. Rolling was all he did, pounding out round after round, working three different pastry boards at once as Liz supplied dough balls and transferred finished rounds to the grills.

"I just wanted to find a church I could love, and a church that would love me, too," he said after finishing one round and moving to another pastry board. "Hawk Creek called me, and here I am. And we've been loving each other ever since."

I asked if Hawk Creek is the church that lefse built—and would build again after the fire. Dan smiled.

"I don't think anyone has joined the church because of the Lefse Ministry, but the ministry has created a whole different spirit. We've found something we enjoy doing together, and it has changed the mood from a church that said, 'We're just a small church that can't do anything. How long are we going to last? Are we going to be able to survive another 10 years?' We moved from those kinds of questions to a realization that as a small church we can make a huge difference."

Before the Lefse Ministry, Dan explained, Hawk Creek was known as the church where a man committed suicide. A murderer running from the law shot himself and was found dead on the church basement floor. But with Dan's missionary drive, Hawk Creek is now known as the church with the Lefse Ministry.

"You see, in many cases our ancestors built churches before they even built their own homes and their schools," said Dan. "For them, their church was their highest priority, and the sacrifices people made in order to fund the building and activities of the church were amazing.

"Most of today's churches are losing members. In our area, there are fewer farmers, and the rural population in general is going down. So it's a challenge to grow a church. And yet last May, we celebrated 23 new members."

Liz, lifting a round as Dan moved on to a board with a dough ball on it, chimed in. "How much did lefse contribute to that?" she asked. "None. But lefse making is one way to work together and to provide some hope. People have to have hope. Nobody is going to join a church that has no hope."

"Bonked" by Fire

My final visit was with Joyce, the coordinator who had been wearing many hats that day and was now helping with packaging. "People are amazed that a little country church can pull this off," she said. "We get participation from 35 to 40 percent of our membership. Yes, the fundraising part is great, but what makes it a ministry for me is having the prayers in the packages."

"How much money do you raise?" I asked.

"We make $3,000 to $4,000 that goes toward the general fund or for special projects like a new furnace, new elevator, or to redo the kitchen. That's why it was so heartbreaking when Hawk Creek burned down. We put a lot into the church in the last 10 years or so."

"What has been the effect on the congregation?" I asked. "Having your church burn to the ground is a huge loss."

Joyce Bigaouette, filling lefse orders, says Hawk Creek church's burning "bonked" everybody up so 35 to 40 percent of membership participated in the lefse-making festival.

"Amazingly, it kinda just *bonked* everybody up," Joyce said. "We've been blessed with a wonderful congregation. It's been growing, and we have a lot of young people. I would say 10 or 12 years ago, we considered closing Sunday school because we only had a handful of kids. Right now we have 30 to 40 kids in Sunday school. A lot of it is Pastor Dan. I don't know many pastors who get down on their haunches every Sunday morning and hug every little kid that leaves church. And there are older kids, 8- and 9-year-olds, who still come by wanting a hug."

"What would happen to the Lefse Ministry if Dan were to leave?"

Joyce shook her head as if banishing the thought. "He's a big part of this," she said. "We couldn't do it without him. And he just loves it, to see how many he can get done in the shortest amount of time. We don't get as many young people for the lefse making as we'd like, however. We were joking the other day that in 10 years we'll have to *lower* the tables because we'll all be in wheelchairs. Oh, you gotta have a sense of humor!"

*Pass it on to one another/Sharing love is the way/
Say thanks, keep the faith, you'll be OK.*

—lyrics to "Keep On Rollin'"

PROFILED AS A LEFSE ROLLER

You have to think big when you think of Mark Bigaouette, a member of the production crew for the Hawk Creek Lefse Ministry. He has a big smile, a big bass voice, and a big heart—and he's a big-time lefse roller. Here are the highlights of my somewhat peculiar conversation with Mark.

Legwold: *How did you get into rolling lefse?*
Mark: Until I met my wife, Joyce, I had never heard of lefse. When they started Hawk Creek's lefse making, I got put into the rolling role right off the bat. They never questioned me about being French and German. They just said, "Good, we have another roller."

Legwold: *How did they know you were a roller?*
Mark: My size. I got profiled. I'm 6-0 and 310 pounds. I'm tall and can put my weight behind it.

Legwold: *Why do you like doing this?*
Mark: Because it makes people happy. I like to help and see people smile.

Legwold: *Wait, you've seen Scandinavians smiling? There's been a sighting?*
Mark: It's a rare form of smiling. I've seen it in my relatives, who are all Norwegian. I've seen it in some of my coworkers.

Legwold: *C'mon, they actually smile?*
Mark: A crack, a little smile. You don't want to go ear to ear.

Legwold: *Has anyone broken down and gone ear to ear?*
Mark: I brought a tray of buttered and sugared lefse into the office, and I stopped by a cowork-er's desk. She couldn't contain herself. It was like, "Whoops!" I said,

Mark Bigaouette, lefse roller.

"Gotcha!" Lucky for her it was in a private office. What would have happened had it been in public?

Legwold: *She worried word would get out about this slip?*
Mark: She said, "You're not going to say anything, are you?" I said, "No."

Legwold: *What is your job?*
Mark: I'm a chemical dependency counselor at Project Turnabout in Granite Falls. We work with people with ad-dictions—compulsive gamblers, alcoholics, drug addicts. This year my coworkers ordered close to 50 packages of lefse. Scandinavian or not, everybody seems to like lefse.

Legwold: *How is recovery like lefse making?*
Mark: They are both life-changing experiences. Once you get into recovery from addiction, you don't go back. And once you get into making lefse, you can never go back.

22
An Original Lefse Song

My grandmother Tora Tviberg Norheim was an excellent teacher and would sing little songs while she did her lefse rolling. It made us kids smile.

—Sally Norheim Dwyer, 62, Petersburg, Alaska

Elida Peterson was the first lefse maker to inspire the song that premieres in this chapter. For *The Last Word on Lefse,* 1 interviewed Elida 25 years ago in her place in Good Shepherd Community Apartments in Rushford, Minnesota. 1 wrote: "It was early evening and she had just finished making lefse that afternoon. For Christmas that year she was giving three dozen lefse to each of her six grown children. ... She was selling lefse again that year at Christmas, and the phone rang as we sat at the table. Ya, she would take their order."

The story continued: "Even reaching up to answer the phone was hard for Elida. She had arthritis bad in her hip and had had two knee replacements. When she shifted her weight on the pillows on her chair, she just had to pause and gulp down the pain.

"'I think this is going to be my last year making lefse,' she said, with a sigh. 'And without lefse, it won't be Christmas. I've always had lefse at Christmas. Always.'

"Sure it would be tough to give it up, she admitted, but what could she do? The pain, you know. The phone rang again. Ya, Mildred, but not a dozen. Elida would make her six rounds of lefse, and that would be it."

Resiliency. That's what was impressive about Elida, that and her passion for tradition. Lefse was fundamental to her holiday, so she had decided to keep on rolling in spite of the arthritis and knee replacements. While some apartments in assisted-care facilities have a lonely, sterile, and, frankly, forlorn feel to them, Elida's home smelled of lefse—and her phone was ringing. She was wanted, in demand, appreciated. She still had it, that magic in her rolling touch.

Two other examples of resiliency from *The Last Word on Lefse*: Ida Saquitne still had it, rolling at age 90 in her apartment in Decorah, Iowa. And Herb and Anna Solem from Spring Grove, Minnesota, still made lefse after Herb's stroke. Sometimes, while Anna rolled, Herb would cry because he couldn't grill the way he had before the stroke. But some days he still had it, and they'd pass the lefse stick back and forth between them just like old times.

During my travels for this book, I met Biddy Seim. At her farm south of Detroit Lakes, Minnesota, 89-year-old Biddy rolls lefse in spite of her curled, arthritic hands. She's had open-heart surgery, a mastectomy, hips redone, and operations on her feet. "But I'm not going to stop just because it gets a little harder," she said. "Lefse making is just something we do."

Joyce Schmidt, 88, keeps on rolling lefse and making huge holiday meals all by herself in Strum, Wisconsin. Millie and Cal Moen, in their 90s, are still striving for first place in the National Lefse Cook-off in Barnesville, Minnesota. Morrie Howland of Ortonville, Minnesota, kept on rolling until the end of his life, winning the national cook-off three times in his 90s. And the day I met him at age 96, he was determined to roll eight rounds—even while recovering from cancer and bouts of pneumonia.

And when lefse makers can't roll anymore, their resiliency still shines on. Hazel Larsgaard stopped rolling lefse in her 90s but kept rolling through the seasons until she died at age 101, thankful for every day and an inspiration to her family. "Gotta live your life right, then you're OK," she'd say.

Finally, my mentor Linda Bengtson from Northfield, Minnesota, no longer rolls, but she keeps on rolling with an attitude of gratitude that transcends the pain from rheumatoid arthritis. She has limited mobility but stays engaged, remembering birthdays and special occasions with handwritten notes and surprising the family with blessings, humor, and out-of-the-blue gifts. She invariably says thanks for whatever kindness comes her way.

And so, these and many other lefse makers inspired my new song, "Keep On Rollin'," which is about resiliency, gratitude, and faith.

Why Write an Original Lefse Song?

The short answer: Why not? I love music and singing and lefse, so why not write a love song about all three? Plus, winding up a heartfelt book with a lefse postlude is a good way to go out. I did that with *The Last Word on Lefse,* ending with the lyrics to "I'll Be Home for Lefse" by LeRoy Larson and the Minnesota Scandinavian Ensemble. I also borrowed lyrics from the most famous lefse song of all, "Just a Little Lefse Will Go a Long Way," by Stan Boreson and Doug Setterberg. The chorus to their song starts with these lines:

> *Just a little lefse will go a long way.*
> *Gives you indigestion most all of the day …*

Lefse has certainly inspired other lyricists. Merlin Hoiness told me he didn't know who wrote the lyrics to two songs he included in his cookbook *91 Ways To Serve Lefse.* The first was "Oh Ya You Betcha," sung to the tune of "Deep in the Heart of Texas." It opens with these lines:

> *The lefse's round with spots of brown*
> *Oh ya you betcha, uff da …*

The second was a lefse lover's "Deck the Halls," which opens with:

Deck the halls with lefse slices, fa la la la la la la uff da
Do not check on what the price is, fa la la la la la la uff da
Might be thought a strange creation, fa la la la la la la la la
But it's great as insulation, fa la la la la la la uff da ...

Red Stangland's *Norwegian Home Companion* includes "The Lefse Song," which is sung to the tune of "Camptown Races." Stangland doesn't attribute it to anyone, so he was probably the lyricist. It begins:

Norsky ladies sing this song, Uff Da. Uff Da.
Bake that lefse all day long, all the Uff Da day.
Bake it till it's almost brown, Uff Da. Uff Da.
Makes you jump just like a clown, all day Uff Da day ...

Last but not least, for *The Last Word on Lefse,* I wrote "Iss Called Lefse for a Purpose," which is sung to the Mac Davis tune "It's Hard to Be Humble." These are the lyrics:

O Lord it iss hard to make lefse
Dat iss perfect in every vay.
To roll dem so round and so tin
Ha, ha, ha, ho, ho—dat vill be da day!
To know lefse, ya sure, iss to love it
No matter how tick, tough, or dead.
And if lefse vas s'pose to be yust right
Ve'd call lefse "yust rightse" instead.

So back to the question: Why write an original lefse song? To use a golfing expression (which I've used too many times after teeing off): "The fairway is wide open." It means everyone else in your foursome has teed off before you and missed the fairway, which you can land in all by your lonesome with a good drive. There aren't that many lefse songs, and those that are available, including mine, miss the mark, in my opinion. Some lefse songs are cute and campy, but the music, with a couple of exceptions, is not original.

How to Write an Original Lefse Song

I've not written music and don't know music well enough to try. As a choir singer and sometime soloist, I've studied songs that I've sung and changed the lyrics when I felt they needed changing or written lyrics for a new verse. But to write music, actual notes in the treble and bass clefs that sound good together? Nope, I needed a pro.

Turns out lots of composers live in the Twin Cities area, and several belong to my church, Mayflower Congregational United Church of Christ in Minneapolis. So I have spent many enjoyable hours hearing how these musicians compose a score. What was their process, and what would they advise for writing "Keep On Rollin'," my proposed song? Here are a few of their suggestions:

Dorothy Williams, Mayflower's organist: Pay attention to the number of words. "Usually, there are way, way, way too many words for a song," said Dorothy. She advised to come up with the "hook," that precious key phrase or passage that drives home the meaning of the song. Don't clutter up this message with a lot of extra words, she advised. Let the simple message shine with supporting music.

Or ...

If the message gets wordy, simplify the music. She wrote the music to "Positive," based on a complex poem by Deborah Keenan. The poem is about receiving a positive diagnosis of AIDS. It was written in the early days of the disease when such a diagnosis meant shame and usually early death. "I was trying to relate the gravitas of all that, but yet come out and say, 'We're here. We're still here. We can be HIV-positive and yet still be positive about life,'" explained Dorothy. "With so many words,

Dorothy Williams advises songwriters not to clutter up their message with too many words. Keep it simple, she says, and let the music support your well-chosen words.

I couldn't have a complicated harmony. I had to keep it focused and stripped down, so the words shined. Basically, I just wrote the music to support the words, to be a vehicle for delivering the words."

Nancy Grundahl, Mayflower's director of music: Nancy said she needs to find a compelling text, "and then I go for a walk," she said. "I walk and sing and try different things, and then I might come home and write it down. I live with that for an hour, two hours, or two days, and try it again."

Nancy Grundahl says songwriters who sing have an advantage when composing.

Nancy has had 75 of her choral pieces published. She composed "Oh Be Swift To Be Kind" in 2016, shortly after the fatal shooting of Philando Castile, a black man from St. Paul, by Jeronimo Yanez, a police officer from St. Anthony, Minnesota. "Music helps expression," said Nancy. "Grief is pretty hard to express in words. Like you say to someone who is grieving, 'I have no words.'

"Music expands the moment. When you have a powerful statement, you can make it last longer in time with music. You can make the rhythm longer. You can sing it longer. You can repeat it, change keys, and repeat it later. That's different than when you read a statement. Once you read it, it's done. Usually, there's just that one time."

Nancy's best advice: "A good song is something that sings well, so songwriters who sing sometimes have an advantage. They know what feels good to sing, what their body likes to do. If I were to pat myself on the back for anything, it's that I write stuff that feels good to sing because I am a singer. So, I would start right away with what feels good to sing."

David Carey, tenor in Mayflower's choir, producer, director, and actor: David would call himself a songwriter only reluctantly, but he has written songs for commercial use as well as for Mayflower ensembles and soloists. One of my favorites is "On the Road," which has a beautiful melody and a simple Easter message of laying down your palm branches.

"When you write a song, you step out of reality and into music," David said. Ideas for a song may be grounded in reality, but those ideas are released by music and come to life in unpredictable ways. Because of this unpredictability, he said, don't settle when ideas come. Be inquisitive and patient. Wait for other ideas. Spend time doodling, staring, plunking on the piano, and listening to the competing voices in your head. Don't dismiss way-out ideas; sometimes they spark a way-cool idea. Try various approaches to expressing your ideas. After a spell of internal back-and-forth brainstorming, ideas eliminate themselves or come up short when compared with a strong message that persists in your thinking. "When I'm writing a song, that's how my brain works," said David. "It's having a conversation with itself."

He put the songwriting process in a nutshell. "Start with the question: 'What's the notion I'm getting at?' When you answer that, you'll find the hook, which is usually in the chorus and the words. The hook is the one thing that repeats, that people will remember, and is probably in the name of the song. Once you have the hook, this usually puts you in an environment where you say, 'I hear the music. I hear what kind of music will be with that message'—it's a guitar slowly strumming, or whatever it is. The music will *feel* right for the message. And that's when the melody starts to feed in."

David Carey counsels songwriters to be patient and not settle for their first ideas.

A parting bit of advice from David: Use your sense of humor, when appropriate, in the lyrics. Listeners and performers love the lift that humor can provide. David's daughter, Marin, went to the Minnesota State Fair when she was 14 and came home with a story about the Pronto Pup boy. "There was this really cute teenage boy that kept looking at her and smiling," said David, "so I wrote a song called 'The Pronto Pup Boy.' My favorite part in the chorus goes, 'Pronto Pup boy, blue eyes and blonde hair, you stole my heart that day at the fair. I'd give you my heart if age didn't matter, and watch you all day dip that dog in that batter.'"

Marty Haugen says he no longer worries about wasting creative time.

Marty Haugen, Mayflower member and liturgical composer: "There was a long time in my professional life when I would sit for two or three hours and nothing would happen," said Marty. "I'd say, 'Boy, this was a wasted morning.' I don't say that anymore. I think sitting there is part of the process now. For me, it takes real patience, sitting and waiting, because it doesn't automatically come on demand. And even when it does, you don't know for some time whether it's any good or not. You need to spend time with it and have others spend time with it."

Marty had recently written 14 different settings of an immigrant piece, "In These Times," before settling on one. He played four of these settings in a workshop on composing, and asked the group for feedback. "They chose one setting that I had not put at the top of my list," Marty said. "So you don't know."

He said lyrics are different from poetry. "Lyrics have to fit. You have to try to say as much as you can with as few words as possible. That's the nature of lyrics. You can't run on and on, because it won't fit to music."

With few words to work with, they have to be spot-on. Marty quoted Mark Twain: "The difference between the almost right word and the right word is really a large matter—it's the difference between the lightning bug and the lightning."

"The words we sing affect us," said Marty, "so you want to be very careful about what you ask other people to sing. It's one thing to say something together as a community—to recite a prayer or a poem—but it's a totally different thing when people sing it together. The whole emotional and unification level goes up a notch when people sing together as opposed to speaking together."

In sum, choose words with deliberation because words will point to the melody, and melody will bring in the supporting arrangement. The end result is often a powerful words-music combination that will find the soul. Marty said, "There's a passage in the Bible where Paul says, 'The cries and groans of the spirit too deep for words.' I think music is deeper than words. Music is a language just like any other language, but it's a language of the heart rather than the head."

Stop Talking, Start Writing

Thus, with my head full of words of advice and a song title in mind, I asked around about songwriters and found St. Paul composer Erik Sherburne to write the score. I told Erik I wanted to include an original lefse-type song in my new book. The title would be "Keep On Rollin'," and the song would honor Elida Peterson–type resiliency and the value of tradition.

"I am intrigued, partially because I'm Norwegian," said Erik, when we met over lunch. "I mean, Sherburne's an English name, and I'm also German and a little bit of everything. But immediately my thoughts go to my wife's family, which is 100-percent Norwegian. They have these big family reunions, and lefse is certainly part of most holiday meals."

Erik said when he first went to this family reunion, his in-laws made him wear lefse, buttered, on top of his bald head as an initiation rite. He did so and felt the door to family acceptance open a bit. However, he had a hunch that writing a lefse song could kick that door wide open.

"There's always music going on in my head," Erik said of his writing process. "It's like my life has a soundtrack. I'll sketch out the song, either singing into the recorder on my phone, or writing on staff paper that's stashed in my wallet, in my car, or at work. Songwriting is like finding a treasure. You're finding this thing and releasing it to the world to do with as it sees fit. People may like it or not like it—that's up to them. That doesn't necessarily bother me. I'm grateful just to have the opportunity to get it out of my head."

Not Settling

The first few versions that came out of Erik's head were in 3/4 time, a waltz. He came up with the line "Embrace the tradition, the passage of time," and I thought, "Cool! We're on the right track." But after a while we realized that, although the time signature fit well with the words and the motion of rolling lefse, the song wasn't doing much for either of us.

We could have made something out of a waltz tune, but Erik was relieved when I suggested switching to 4/4 time. Let's make the song a statement, not a dance. And while we're at it, let's try writing in some gospel and blues, which we both like. The song wouldn't be pure Norwegian, but in the end we had to feel it. In the conversations my brain was having with itself, the most dominant voice lobbied that gospel feels good to sing and is all about resiliency and the imploring command: "Keep On Rollin'."

"Cool!" I thought. "Now, we're *really* on the right track."

Uh, not quite. Erik was coming up with lovely, intriguing melodies, but the song had no story to go with the hook of "Keep On Rolling." Erik used notes from our conversations and emails to come up with lines in the chorus and verses, but they amounted to what Dorothy would call "spaghetti," words that wound around and didn't go anywhere.

It was time for me to write the story. I sat with the scraps we had for a song so far, as Nancy suggested. I doodled and stared. I went for a run. I ate and went to bed, grumpy that I wasn't getting anywhere but trusting that what appeared to be time "wasted," as Marty said, was an important part of the process.

I awoke the next day and, as is my custom, said a prayer for faith.

Each evening I say a prayer of gratitude for the day that's ended, and the following morning I say a prayer for faith for the day to come. ... Wait! Is that it? The more I thought about it, the more I saw that gratitude and faith feed and strengthen resiliency.

I was *feeling* this connection, but still, where did lefse come in? "Keep On Rollin'" will appear in a book about lefse, Gary, not in a ruminative, religious tome. I didn't have an answer, but, buoyed by David's brilliant ramblings on brainstorming, I decided to plunge ahead anyway and not toss this idea. David had said

Composer Erik Sherburne enjoys the discovery process in songwriting.

songwriting was about stepping out of reality and into music, so maybe music had the answer.

One other key point I learned about songwriting: It's OK to "steal." This is *not* plagiarizing. David said flat out that Erik and I were not going to create a new piece of art; everything's been done. But it's common for songwriters to pay tribute to great artists like Randy Newman and Leonard Cohen by using something from their body of work. "I'm talking about this one thing that you know will resonate with the listener," David said. "You're stealing not from another *song* but from something bigger, something you know listeners will connect with."

"What you learn is you are not Mozart, not Bach," said Marty. "The world doesn't rise or fall on what you write. You are imperfect and what you write will be imperfect, but it doesn't mean you should slough off or do anything less than your best."

Running Down the Lyrics

To a perfectionist like me, the inevitability of imperfection was a huge green light—to hear and accept the lyrics I wrote. I would do my best, but the result wouldn't be perfect. So lighten up.

I went for a Saturday morning run and through my earbuds

listened to National Public Radio's Scott Simon interview BJ Leiderman, who has composed theme music for radio programs such as *Morning Edition* and *Weekend Edition*. The interview included a sound bite from Leiderman's inspiring new song "Praise One Another." I stopped running to listen. This was the type of song, powerfully joyful, I wanted "Keep On Rollin'" to be. The lyrics to the chorus of his song are:

Praise one another.
Worship one another.
Love one another and the whole round world will be fine.

I sang the "Praise One Another" chorus for a few days and reflected on all that was packed into that musical bundle. And then I sat to write lyrics for "Keep On Rollin'."

I worked on the chorus first. Erik had written the lines:

Keep on rollin'
Keep on rollin'
Keep on rollin' and make traditions shine
Keep on rollin'
Keep on rollin'

So I needed a line to finish off the chorus. With faith and gratitude in mind, I added: *Keep the faith, oh give thanks, and you'll be fine.*

It wasn't perfect, but it said what I wanted—and believed—in just a few words.

Once I felt on solid ground with the chorus, the verses were fun and fairly fast to write. One verse would be on sharing, which is a form of faith; you're likely to share when you know you'll have enough. Another verse would be on faith, and the third would be on gratitude.

But what about lefse? "Keep on rollin' and make traditions shine" was about lefse and sharing. It applied to giving away rounds of lefse at the holidays and sharing recipes and know-how with beginners. But the song could use more lefse. (What doesn't need more lefse?)

This is where the bridge would help. A song's bridge typically causes the listener to pause and reflect on what has been sung so far; it can also serve to prepare the listener for the climax. Maybe there was a way to work lefse into the bridge.

While driving on the Lefse Trail, I would fill the time composing short, sometimes silly lefse poems like this:

> *Every batch a drama*
> *Just like every day*
> *Will things turn out alright?*
> *You know, you'll find a way.*
> > *Just keep on rolling.*

> *Ooga-baga-biga-baga*
> *Biga-baga-boo*
> *You love lefse*
> *And I love you*
> > *Yep, keep on rolling.*

I gave a mess of these poems to Erik, hoping he could fashion a bridge out of them. He tried but it was really my job to write more lefse into the song, in the bridge or maybe in a verse. In a pivotal late-evening phone conversation, he challenged me to think about the original intent of the song and to shake things up and see what happened. Maybe make a bridge out of a verse I had discarded and somehow write lefse and faith into a new verse?

I hung up relieved and woke the next morning eager to rewrite. Writing is rewriting, right? I tried what Erik suggested, and it worked. Not perfectly, but it worked and felt great to sing. The last thing I did was shorten some of the lefse poems into three-line, call-and-response ditties. The result made for a fun break between the verses and a buildup to the ending.

Erik and I fiddled with this and that many, many, many times, and I sent the "final" to Dorothy and Nancy, who provided minor tweaks and congratulations. There are still spots that have their issues, but Erik and I finally came up with a song we were pleased with. So with all that—undoubtedly the longest introduction to a lefse song ever—here is "Keep On Rollin'" for you!

An Original Lefse Song

Keep On Rollin'

Lyrics by: Gary Legwold

Music by: Erik Sherburne

Keep On Rollin'

ceive   Keep on   a   roll - in'   you'll have e - nough I   do be - lieve There's
where   Keep on   a   roll - in'   So bleak out-side __ but   you don't care

plen - ty here   for   you and me __ Now's the time to start   So just   o - pen   your
Ev' - ry batch   a   dra - ma __ Just like ev' - ry day   Keep on   roll - in'   you

e - ver lov - in' __ heart   Keep on roll - in'   Keep on roll - in'
know you'll find a __ way

Keep On Rollin'

Keep On Rollin'

Keep On Rollin'

tall   be   true   stay strong   be   you!"

Up tempo and fun ♩ = 88

f   1.Get it thin__ go light on the pin__ [And Keep   On   Roll - in']
2.Trust the dough roll nice - and slow__

Turn that round Get it toa - sty brown [And Keep   On   Roll - in']   Give thanks to your

Keep On Rollin'

6

Keep On Rollin'

roll - in'   Keep on   roll - in'   Keep on   roll - in'   and

let tra - di - tion   shine   Keep on   roll - in'   Keep on

ro - llin' keeep the faith, and give your thanks   faith and give your

Keep On Rollin'

8

thanks   Keep   faith _____   give   thanks   you'll   be

fine! _____

23
The "Last" Word on Lefse

*When I teach someone to make lefse,
here's what I say: "Now you have to teach
somebody else—and keep it rolling."*

—Nolan Spencer, 77, Deerwood, Minnesota

When I was younger, about the time *The Last Word on Lefse* was published, I went to the Boundary Waters Canoe Area Wilderness in northern Minnesota and hiked part of the Border Route Trail. This 65-mile-long trail crosses the BWCAW and traces the line between Minnesota and Ontario, Canada. It is known as a rugged wilderness trail that follows ridgelines and the tops of high cliffs and thus offers expansive views across the Boundary Waters and Quetico Provincial Park.

I hiked alone on a marvelous autumn day, looking out at the views and in at my soul, reflecting on the big questions of life and grateful for the simplicity that hiking offers. Walk. Rest. Drink. Eat. Smile. Repeat.

I came to Rose Lake's iconic overlook, a favorite of photographers. I snapped off a couple of shots, knowing they would not do the scene justice. Wisely, I just put the camera away, removed my hat in reverence, and took in the moment. The visuals were what you'd expect from a gorgeous lake *waaaaaaaay* down below, and from being able to see other lakes and ridges *waaaaaaaay* far away. They were not to be taken for granted that day, and in gratitude I just stood and stared for I don't know how long. I tried to fix the scene in my head, the curve of the lakes, the winking of the sun's reflection off the waves, the trees that shot up impossibly from seemingly barren slanting slabs of granite.

I started crying at the beauty of it all, and it felt good to let it go. I was crying in gratitude but also in grief, that it would be the last time I would have this view. I didn't visit the Boundary Waters often and knew, with so much of the world to see, I would not return, at least to this particular spot.

I had my cry and said a prayer, and I resumed hiking. It was time to go home.

I had hiked maybe five minutes when I realized I was missing my hat. It had to be back at the Rose Lake vista. So I did an about-face and walked back. Sure enough, my hat was right where I put it when I was in my meditation. I picked it up and put it on, and I couldn't help but take in the scene. I shook my head. I was enjoying the very view that ten minutes earlier I was so sure I would never see again. A voice inside my head said, "People plan and God smiles."

Well, I had to smile as I enjoyed my Rose Lake moment one "last" time. What did I know? I set off walking one step at a time, grinning at each hiker approaching the overlook.

After writing *The Last Word on Lefse,* I knew I would never write another book about lefse. One was enough. What more could I say? And yet here I am.

I cry now because I will miss the ongoing discovery that comes with writing about something dear and cherished, something like lefse. When I am writing on matters near to my heart, I am with God.

I also grin at this book, at where it has taken me. Books are like children; they lead us to unpredictable places—and we are the better for it (usually). This book has led me along the Lefse Trail, visiting old friends and making new ones—friends who also have a thing for lefse, who understand perfectly well why someone would write two books on this simple-yet-saintly food. I have learned from each of them at lefse fests, over savory lefse wraps, and in church basements. I have learned how to make a handsome lefse rolling pin that I will pass on to my children. And by writing lyrics to an original lefse song, I have learned about the emotional power of combining words with music. "Keep the faith, O give thanks, and you'll be fine."

Finally, I have learned there is no last word on lefse. I once feared the lefse-making tradition would die off. It may, but I'm not too worried about that anymore. Based on 25 years of looking at all things lefse, my sense is lefse making is picking up, not winding down. It goes on and on.

So, having learned from my Rose Lake experience, I won't say I'm done writing about lefse. What do I know? And I won't say that there is a last word on lefse. However, if pressed to come up with some sort of benediction, I would say this:

Keep on rolling.

Appendix

Photo Guide to Making Potato Lefse

In addition to a lefse rolling pin and lefse grill, here's what you need to make potato lefse.

There are many types of lefse and many ways to make it. This is my way and my recipe, presented in this photo tutorial for those who do not know how to make potato lefse and are eager to learn. Enjoy!

3	cups riced potatoes (about 8 medium-size potatoes, russets preferred, never reds)
5	tablespoons melted salted butter
½	teaspoon salt
1	tablespoon powdered sugar
¼	cup cream
1¼–1½ cups flour to mix with dough, extra for spreading on rolling surface and rolling pin	

Makes about 10 lefse

1. *First, scrub your spuds.*

2. *Boil potatoes with skin on to add flavor to lefse.*

3. *When potatoes are done, pour off hot water.*

4. *Put boiled potatoes in a bowl for mashing.*

5. *Peel the thin skin from your boiled potatoes.*

6. *Mash your peeled potatoes.*

7. *Rice your potatoes. Twice is nice.*

8. *Pack 3 cups of riced potatoes and put in a mixing bowl.*

9. *Stir salt and sugar into melted butter.*

10. *Pour sugar-salt-butter mixture into riced potatoes.*

11. *Add cream to the potato mix.*

12. *Mix cream thoroughly into dough.*

13. *Cover dough and let cool. Most lefse makers cool the dough overnight in a refrigerator, but some don't and roll with slightly warm dough.*

14. *Get ready to roll! Preheat the lefse grill, and spread flour on your rolling surface.*

15. *Knead flour into the dough right before rolling.*

16. *Shape your lefse patty, taking care that there are no cracks in the edge.*

17. *Start rolling and go light on the pin.*

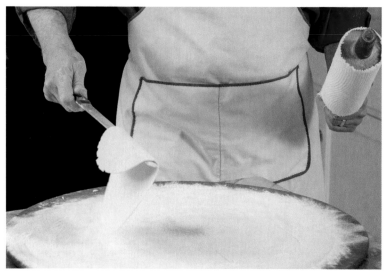

18. *To prevent the round from sticking, turn it over when rolled to about half the intended size.*

19. *Roll out your round, lifting your pin at the edges so they don't get too thin and crisp on the grill.*

20. Once your round is rolled to the size and thinness you desire, use a lefse stick to lift it to the grill.

21. When bubbles form, flip your round. Undercook side A to retain moisture in your lefse. Make side B your "show" side by grilling until beautiful brown spots appear.

22. *Finally, roll until your dough is gone. Practice, improve, and appreciate the beauty—and flavor—of each round. Then rest assured: You are a lefse maker!*